# A-Level Business

# CloudLearn Ltd

**Specification code: 9BS0**

**First Teaching: 2015**

**First Assessment: 2017**

A Level Business

Published and distributed by: OSC Ltd.

First published in July 2015

Edition Number: 2015/01

Disclaimer

The authors of this text believe the contents of this course to be accurate and correct. While all possible care has been taken in producing this work, no guarantee can be given.

# Contents

# Introduction

You have chosen to study A-Level Business. In order to successfully complete the A-Level Business course from Edexcel, you will need to pass the three A-Level written examinations. You can register to sit these at any examination centre that will accept you as an external candidate, and we remind you that it is your responsibility to find an examination centre and to book your exams.

# Assessment

In this course, at the end of certain topics, you will find a series of TMAs (Tutor Marked Assignments). The answers should be types onto a word document and uploaded to your tutor for marking when you reach the appropriate place.

Throughout the course there are a number of activities and self-assessment questions: these are **not** to be returned to your tutor. They are there to get you thinking about key concepts and ideas and to encourage you to do some on-going revision and additional research as and when needed.

In order to sit your exams you will need to contact an examination centre and organise this for yourselves.

Details of the written exams can be found on the following page.

Please note with regard to paper three that there is a ore-release booklet of information for that exam which will be sent to you by your examination centre (not by us) several weeks prior to the exam. You must liaise with your exam centre on when this will be delivered.

# Core Content

The A-Level Business consists of 4 themes:

Theme 1 – Marketing and People

Theme 2 – Managing Business Activities

Theme 3 – Business Decisions and Strategy

Theme 4 – Global Business

The formal assessment for A-Level Business is as follows:

Students must complete all assessment in May/June in any single year.

| Paper 1: Marketing, people and global businesses | |
|---|---|
| | *Paper code: 9BS0/01 |
| • Externally assessed<br>• Availability: May/June<br>• First assessment: 2017 | 35% of the total qualification |
| **Overview of content**<br>Paper 1 will assess marketing, people and global businesses. Questions will be drawn from Themes 1 and 4, and from local, national and global contexts. | |
| **Overview of assessment**<br>• Written examination.<br>• The paper comprises two sections.<br>• Students answer all questions from both sections.<br>• Sections A and B each comprise one data response question broken down into a number of parts, including one extended open-response question.<br>• Duration: 2 hours.<br>• 100 marks available. | |

| Paper 2: Business activities, decisions and strategy | |
|---|---|
| | *Paper code: 9BS0/02 |
| • Externally assessed<br>• Availability: May/June<br>• First assessment: 2017 | 35% of the total qualification |

**Overview of content**

Paper 2 will assess business finance and operations, business decisions and strategy. Questions will be drawn from Themes 2 and 3, and from local, national and global contexts.

**Overview of assessment**

- Written examination.
- The paper comprises two sections.
- Students answer all questions from both sections.
- Sections A and B each comprise one data response question broken down into a number of parts, including one extended open-response question.
- Duration: 2 hours.
- 100 marks available.

## Paper 3: Investigating business in a competitive environment

**\*Paper code: 9BS0/03**

| | |
|---|---|
| • Externally assessed<br>• Availability: May/June<br>• First assessment: 2017 | **30% of the total qualification** |

### Overview of content

Paper 3 will assess content across all four themes. Questions will be drawn from local, national and global contexts.

For Paper 3, there will be a pre-released context document issued on our website in November of the previous year. A new context will be given to centres each year and will relate to the examination series for the following summer.

The context will focus on a broad context, such as an industry or market in which businesses operate. The question paper will be in two sections.

The first section will focus on the broad context provided. This will be outlined to centres through the pre-released document. Questions will focus on the broad context.

The second section will focus on at least one strand within the context provided, such as a particular business.

Each section will contain unseen stimulus materials comprising quantitative and qualitative evidence. Students are required to apply their knowledge and understanding from Themes 1, 2, 3 and 4 and their understanding of the broad context to this evidence.

Students cannot take any of their research or investigation data carried out as part of the pre-release into the examination.

### Overview of assessment

- Written examination.
- The paper comprises two sections.
- Students answer all questions from both sections.
- Sections A and B each comprise one data response question broken down into a number of parts, including one extended open-response question.
- Duration: 2 hours.
- 100 marks available.

# Timescales

The written exams are held in May/June every year (starting in 2017).

You need to confirm the specific dates with your chosen examination centre, and we always recommend you book your exams early.

Students must take all written exams in the same year; it is not permissible to take some exams one year and some the following year.

# Course structure

The course is written systematically to cover the Edexcel specification, and, as a result, there are times when a particular issue or subject is discussed in more than one section. This is not an error but reflects the specification which also does this. This should not in any way harm your learning but should actually enhance it as it gives you the opportunity to learn/revise a key issue in several different areas of the course.

# Theme 1

# Marketing and People

**Introduction**

Theme 1 consists of 5 topics:

- Topic 1.1: Meeting Customer Needs
- Topic 1.2: Market
- Topic 1.3: Marketing Mix and Strategy
- Topic 1.4: Managing People
- Topic 1.5: Entrepreneurs and Leaders

**Topic 1.1 - Meeting Customer Needs**

**Learning Outcome**

The aim of this section is for students to understand the following:

- The Market
- Market Research
- Market Positioning

Electronic markets provide intangible services across geographical boundaries, which makes it a more competitive market. Businesses can provide a wide variety of services over the internet, which allow customers to pay online and not have to physically go into a shop on the high street. Many businesses are tapping into the electronic market, and can generate an immense volume of customers whose needs they can satisfy.

In most markets there is a dominant or mass market of which businesses aim to provide a wide range of good and services which are attractive to a large number of customers.

There are also smaller niche markets that target a specific group of customers by offering a specialised and sometimes unique product or service.

Mass marketing tries to attract customers from all segments of the market and its aim is for businesses to be the market leader and have the most overall sales, which in turn should provide them with the largest market share.

Niche markets have distinct characteristics which include having a fairly small volume of sales which can led to their fixed costs being high. As a consequence the cost of the product or service tends to be high in order to cover the businesses costs. Customers may only be able to acquire the product or service through a limited number of outlets.

Market growth is the percentage incremental increase in the size of a market; for example, we might say a market is growing at 10% per annum.

The market size measures the total sales by businesses that supply products or services to that particular market.

Both market size and market growth can be measured by value and volume.

The measurement by value refers to the growth rate as being determined by the number of units which the business has sold. Measuring the units by value refers to the amount of revenue which the business has generated through these sales.

Economic factors like the interest rate, the price of other similar products and services, disposable income of customers and the rate of inflation can affect the size and growth of a market.

Market share is the proportion of the total market which a specific product or business controls. It is measured by volume or value. The marketing strategy of a business is evaluated by the percentage of market share which it holds.

The market share is usually used by businesses as a tool to evaluate its success or failure. In comparison to its competitors, a business would use the market share position to clearly see who the major performers are or whether or not it is in the same league.

Businesses and individuals offering products and services want to hold as large a share of the market as they possibly can. They look to do this by having branded items. They want customers to think of their products and services before any of their competitors and associate their product with certain characteristics including quality, reliability and value for money. Businesses want to not only attract customers but keep those customers and have repeat business, allowing them to maintain and increase their share of the market.

Traditional markets are changing as society changes and customers tastes and desires move with the latest trends. Markets are moving away from the traditional face-2-face high street stores and are becoming increasingly more online as this overcomes barriers to trade. By trading online businesses can widen their customer base and therefore increase their market share.

Businesses need to remain innovative and try to stay ahead of their competition through anticipating customer's needs and demands and meeting them. This has led businesses to becoming more adaptable and quicker in responding to customers' requirements, in order to stay competitive and also maintain and grow their market share.

**Competition**

This is where two or more businesses supply the same goods or services to the same customers, known as direct competition e.g. coca cola and pepsi. Indirect competition is where businesses make a similar product or service, but compete for the same consumer expenditure. For example, if a person is hungry there are a number of fast food businesses from the consumer to choose from to satisfy this hunger. Therefore a business needs to stand out from the other businesses and become that customer's preferred choice.

Almost all businesses have indirect competition. To remain competitive, the nature of the product/services offered and product range needs to be considered when setting up a new business. The pricing policies and marketing strategy needs to be carefully planned so that the business can compete against other more-well established businesses, within that market.

Competition can be fierce in well established markets with existing business having a stronghold on the market with a large percentage share of that market and loyal customers who repeat buy from that business. Customers can develop a loyalty to a particular business or brand and will choose to buy from that one business over the others within the market. It can be difficult for a new business to gain any credibility or market share with such strong competition. Many businesses fail due to their inability to compete effectively in mature markets with branded and established business already operating.

When businesses are entering into a new market they have the same opportunities as their competition. They need to stand out and offer a product or service that attracts customers to buy from them rather than a competitor. Competition can affect the market as it means that businesses need to offer something that is unique and meets the needs of their customer, in order to gain or maintain market share. Competition can be a positive experience for customers as it allows them more choice and can also create a price war where businesses will undercut one another in order to gain the most number of customers possible.

## Risk and Uncertainty

A risk in business is something that is planned in advance with some probable outcomes which can be considered or at least understood in decision making. An uncertainty is subject to external factors which are outside of the control of the business. For example environmental factors such as tornadoes, floods, Tsunami are sources of uncertainty.

These things can be difficult to predict but businesses need to plan for both eventualities.

Businesses can determine the risk of any decision that they make and minimise that risk through market research and strategic planning. This allows for them to look at all potential outcomes.

The larger the business is, the less the risk involved as the business will have a large market share and may operate in many different markets. This allows the business to take risks, knowing that it has other markets on which it can depend. Business take risks in order to optimise on their potential to both dominate a market and also increase their sales and therefore revenue.

Uncertainty is more difficult to plan for but a business can consider external factors and which ones are likely to impact on the business. For example its geographical location would determine the likelihood of environmental impacts.

Businesses can assess the probability of that situation occurring and put into place strategies and actions in order to address this issue, should it happen.

**Market Research**

**Introduction**

In this section we will look at market research and how it is conducted. In order to provide the best and most useful products and services, a business must know what customers need; this is one of the functions of market research.

There are two main methods of conducting market research:

- Primary research – This is the collection of new data
- Secondary research – This is the use of existing data

Each method has advantages and disadvantages, of course. For this reason, a business must be fully informed of the pros and cons of the methods which they choose for the purposes of conducting market research. Volume and quality are two major factors that are used to decide which methodology is best for any market research project. This introduces the relevance of qualitative and quantitative research, and how these are utilised by market researchers.

Market sampling, sizes and types are needed when focusing on target groups and making sure that the research is most representative of that group audience. There are a number of processes which influence the use of market sampling. There are also risks involved which have to be taken into consideration and carefully avoided.

Once the collation of market research information is complete, the analysis of the information then takes place in stages. The data is thoroughly examined and evaluated through the use of a range of statistical techniques.

**Product and Market Orientation**

A business that prioritises market orientation focuses on providing products for the customer to respond to the needs and wants of the target audience and organise their activities around that. The business will invest in researching trends in the market and produce a strategy to meet the needs and wants of customers. By adapting this focus the business needs to ensure that it is innovative and able to respond quickly to the changing wants and needs of its target market. If a business is unable to do this it can mean that they lose market share to competitors.

Whereas a product orientated businesses focus on the products and the skills and systems that it has in place to support that product. This allows a business to develop the expertise needed to create the products to a high standard and to have highly effective and efficient systems.

**Methods of Primary and Secondary Research**

A business conducts market research to identity relevant information in relation to customers, products and markets.

It is usually necessary for business growth, development and survival to carry out market research regularly because the markets, customers and the business environment are constantly changing.

Through market research, a business can identify its strengths, follow current business trends, seek to enhance available opportunities and improve the areas that it struggles with.

Market research involves collecting information and investigating key factors:

- Future impacts of the environment on business
- The marketing mix
- The overall business environment

Market research can tell you a great deal about the attitude of consumers to your own company and products, information that you might not appreciate or realise.

**Activity 1 – Which do you think is better, primary or secondary research?**

**Primary research**

This process involves gathering new data and generally uses a specialist market research agency in order to conduct the research. The data gathered is now and up to date.

Field research is the mode of collection of primary research information. It requires that the market research agency or employees in the organisation who are involved in the project have to directly interact with the main targets of the market research. Such targets that are needed to participate in the market research project are called the respondents or subjects of the market research.

A lot of time and effort needs to be invested in primary research. Since it is the main focus of the market investigation, every activity involved in the project revolves around the data collected in the field research. Hence, it is important that the information is accurate and reliable.

Typical examples of types of primary research include:

- Focus groups
- Surveys
- Experimentation
- Discussion panels
- Observation
- Field Trials

Focus groups select individuals who meet specific pre-set criteria and invite them for a group conversation. The intention is that they are representative of a larger target audience such as existing or potential business customers, distributors or other members of the business's network, like suppliers and distributors.

Market research agencies use survey tools to gather and collate information for the market research project which they are conducting on behalf of the business.

Surveys could be conducted face-to-face, electronically or via telephone. Surveys target specific groups and use the views and feedback of the respondents to collect relevant data to the market research.

Experimentation uses respondents of a certain targeted group to test out newly developed products or prototypes, before the products are launched to the market.

Discussion panels rely on the expertise of individuals in a particular business field. Through their wealth of knowledge about the field, they provide tremendous experience and valuable input to the research product.

Observation is used to study the behavioural characteristics of the respondents over a period of time. With the use of technological advancements, it can now be done using security/discreet cameras, in addition to face observations.

Field trials follow up on the information gathered from group discussions and actually try out the outcome of the responses.

**Activity 2 – Do you think primary research data is always reliable?**

**Secondary research**

Secondary research makes use of previously collected data which it then uses as the basis of conducting market research.

The findings of this information can then be used for purposes of marketing. Statistical publications are a common form of secondary research.

Published texts including journals, newspapers, magazines, e-zines, and census data are all examples of secondary research data.

There are two types of sources of secondary research data:

- External data – from sources outside of the business
- Internal data – from information which the business possesses such as information on products, sales, customers, accounts

Trade journals, company reports, the internet, universities, libraries and official statistics are sources of external data.

Internal data sources include sales figures, information from products, data records, website monitoring, account records, loyalty schemes and Electronic Point of Sale (EPOS).

**Pros and Cons of Research Methods**

Market research information is very important in assisting businesses in making the best choices to satisfy customers and to stay ahead of the competition.

When properly conducted it accomplishes these objectives and is invaluable. However, it is often the case that data obtained from market research can be inaccurate, misleading and flawed.

When this occurs, the business will receive incorrect information and might develop a business plan that is wholly unsuited to the needs of the customer.

- When mistakes are made, it leads to the making of wrong decisions
- The research data sometimes is not comprehensive and does not reflect the target group
- The choice of market research method can be completely wrong
- Valuable data can be lost because of poor feedback from respondents
- As markets change quickly, research data may easily become obsolete and irrelevant

From technique to technique, unique benefits and limitations apply. A business needs to identify the best method for a specific market research, after careful consideration of its advantages and setbacks.

**Activity 3 – Can you think of any primary market research organisations? Several are often mentioned during election times.**

## Electronic surveys

These are a relatively cheap and time-saving method of collecting market data. Customers and web-site visitors participate in surveys and leave their feedback. It is becoming increasingly popular because of its speed. Yougov is an example of an electronic primary market research organisation.

The major drawback of this method is the lack of controls that the business has over selecting the respondents. In other words, the respondents choose themselves online and can provide false or misleading data for both the criteria for participation selection and the actual survey.

## Focus groups

Focus groups are not very expensive and they are quick to conduct. Individuals who represent a large target market are interviewed and provide valuable information to the business. Focus groups must have good moderators who can clearly build a good rapport with participants, keep the discussion on the right track and monitor progress. In cases where the moderator does not take charge of the discussion, little of use is normally gained.

## Observation

This method of market research is very action-oriented. Whereas a lot of market research pays attention to what people say when they are consciously interviewed, observation studies the behaviours of people without their knowing it; hence the responses are very reliable. There is no pressure on respondents at any time. In addition to that, the subjects of a piece of market research cannot refuse to participate when they do not know they are under observation and inadvertently participating in a market research.

**Surveys**

Surveys are done via telephone, post, and face-to-face.

- Telephone surveys – these have a relatively good rate of response although it can have restrictive questions
- Postal survey – there is no bias from interviewer, it has wide coverage and is less pressurising to respondents. It also is cost-effective. However, the percentage response rate is low and is slow

**Qualitative and Quantitative Research**

**Qualitative research**

Businesses use this method to understand the thought-process that guides customers in their choices and habits when buying products and services. Through evaluating techniques, using data and drawing conclusions from these, the business can understand the decision-making process of customers.

Qualitative research involves the use of focus groups and in-depth interviews. Market researchers can then draw conclusions from the attitudes and behaviours which govern consumer decision-making habits and can form a theory based on their responses.

**Quantitative research**

This method is employed by businesses in making right decisions. It uses formal methods for the purpose of forecasting, measuring and describing quantity through various methods of sampling.

Quantitative research measures a market. It then quantifies the derived measurement with selected data. The data usually relates to the market share, penetration, market size or the growth rate of the market.

Quantitative research gives key insight into the attitudes of customers and their levels of awareness. It assists businesses to understand their customers better.

This research method can target specific market segments and provide important details about such segments. Businesses need to have such details in order to optimise their budgets and make the most of the implemented strategies for marketing products and services.

**Variations between qualitative and quantitative research**

Qualitative and quantitative research are both vital market research methods that focus on strengthening the business decision-making process and understanding the consumers' thinking and behavioural processes. Hence, they vary in several ways as summarised below:

Quantitative research involves greater sample size and reflects the population to a greater extent than qualitative research, which deals with a smaller group.

Quantitative research is less intensive than qualitative research. The interviewer can ask very in-depth questions to secure answers to help the research process.

Quantitative research results are more objective than qualitative results.

In qualitative research, the gathering of data is less rigid than in quantitative research, which tends to be very thoroughly planned.

Motivation, traits of attitudes, and behaviour are understood in greater details when conducting qualitative research.

**Activity 4 – Explain the differences between qualitative and quantitative methods.**

**Samples - Size and Types**

A sample is a selection of a number of people whose views and opinions and considered to be representative of a much larger target group. Samples are required because it is not possible to collect the data of every single person, even though this would be the ideal; however, in practice, it is not very realistic.

A chosen sample group must be reliable, representative and accurate.

The sample size needs to be considered carefully as it is representing a small number out of the total population equally. This is referred to as random sampling. In the course of conducting your own market research, a sample of people is acceptable, as far as the members of the sample can be proven to be representative of the larger target group.

There are two methods used in sampling:

- Probability sampling - Here it is assumed that in the representative population, every individual member has an equal chance of selection to be part of the sample group. Methods of this type of sampling include stratified sampling, random sampling and cluster sampling and systematic sampling
- Non-probability sampling – This is not based on a random selection of members of the sampling. Judgement sampling, convenience sampling, snowball sampling and quota sampling are examples of this type of sampling

**Activity 5 – Why can't you simply choose people off the street to take part in a focus group?**

There are various implications of using sampling methods:

With the use of different types of sampling, there are issues of reliability, cost and accuracy. Random sampling costs tend to be high because of its large nature and scope. It can be time-consuming - both to complete the survey and data collation and analysis of the result.

There are sampling methods chosen as a result of their time-efficiency. For such samples, accuracy is not paramount, and hence the outcomes of such samples are not expected to be very technical and systematic. Whichever method of sampling is used, it should be a reflection of the group targeted for research and must be able to stand up to scrutiny.

**Methods of Sampling and the factors which influence them**

Businesses need to choose the right methods of sampling for market research purposes. In so doing, a number of various factors need to be considered. These include:

Target market - An awareness of who purchases your products or services (i.e. your target market) is vital if the data gathered is to be meaningful. There is usually little point in gathering the thoughts of people who have no interest in your product, although the views of people who might purchase your product are, of course, very important indeed.

Nature of product or service - This is also relevant to the nature of your product. Again, you must be aware of what your product is and who purchases it is you are to gather accurate data from the right people. For example, when research needs to be conducted on specialist products or services, the sample needs to be composed of respondents interested in such products.

Finance - Finance is an important factor in choosing sampling methods. There are expenses to be incurred in conducting market research and these expenses must be worthwhile. In other words, a sampling method selected must produce results and benefits which will be of much greater value to the business and at the same time outweigh the costs used to conduct such research.

Risks involved - The risks involved in the type of sampling would determine whether or not it is practical and effective to engage in such techniques of sampling. A typical example is during the prototype stages and early product development phases. The sampling method used must have respondents who are insightful, knowledgeable and who can add value input to the product prior to its market launch.

**Market Research Data Analysis**

So far we have examined the processes of conducting market research; however, once the information has been collated, then the next stage will be to analyse and evaluate the data, to interpret and apply the results.

There is no standard way of analysing and evaluating data. To a larger extent, the method in which the data was collected determines how it is analysed and evaluated. Simple questionnaires can be analysed and evaluated quickly and easily. Complex questionnaires need more time as they may involve statistical analysis which is costly. With statistical analyses, some analytical methods focus on trends and others focus on information.

Below is a summary of the stages involved in data collation, analysis and evaluation:

- Extracting the information from the questionnaire and compiling all the acquired information into a single document. This is the collation process
- The construction and checking process involves taking the individual questions and graphically representing them by construction of graphs to check the information provided
- Error-checking process involves checking the questionnaires for errors
- The cross-checking and initial presentation need to be followed by another collation process
- Looking at trends, links and patterns in questionnaires, questions and individual questionnaires
- Comparison process which involves comparing raw data with existing data.
- Identifying and highlighting changes, errors and shifts
- Presentation process involves a final presentation of the data in the format which it should be in

The findings of market research can be presented orally, but is more frequently presented as a written report. The recommendation of the market data can be made before the presentation of the findings.

The purposes of recommendations are to give the researchers the opportunity to highlight any new developments as a result of the market research and data collected. These could be new trends or patterns. This is brought to the attention of the business to take relevant action. The recommendations made are done within the framework of the original brief and objectives which it set.

At the end of the process, the business will require answers to certain questions that were fundamental to why the market research was being conducted in the first place.

Any market research recommendation and conclusion must demonstrate that the data gathering and analysis has been scientific and objective, otherwise it is likely to be rejected by the business organisation.

There is also a process of re-evaluation which businesses embark upon to improve their products and services and make them more appealing to the consumers. Once the recommendations and conclusions of the research show that there are areas of the business which need to be improved on, it is in the best interest of the business to quickly improve its products and services to meet the demands of the customers and sustain a formidable market position.

**Types of Market Segmentation**

Now that you understand the concept of a market, let us look at smaller groups within a market, which have similar wants and needs. Businesses come up with a marketing mix which enables them to provide a variety of services for different segments in a market.

Market segments can be categorised into the following groups:

- Family size and type
- Age
- Rate of product use
- Lifestyle
- Location
- Gender

The benefits of market segments include its high level of precision in clearly defining markets. Market segments enable the optimisation of market resources. Market segments are essential because they help discover potential opportunities in the market and how such market gaps can be filled.

Market segmentation has drawbacks which will affect a business. A major drawback is the increase in the cost of production of goods and services. A business may have planned for a specific range or a few set products. However, with different segments, it will have to customise its product to satisfy the demands of those various segments.

Market segments need to be sustainable over a long-period so that the business can have a definite guarantee that it is not in for the short-term and may ultimately stand to lose out in a big way over a long-term period. The ability of market segments to be profitable is important. No business would risk investing in a segment that is not going to bring any valuable returns to the business.

**Market Positioning**

Market mapping is a study of the market conditions of the product or service to identify a gap in the market or to reposition a product or service. The mapping process is plotted on a graph with corresponding variables between consumers and products. This mapping process is particularly useful for new businesses and a business launching a new product or service.

It allows a business to consider its image and if it able to attract and maintain customers for the long term. If the market mapping exercise indicates that the business will have short term gains only, then they can complete a repositioning exercise, which may involve a re-launch with a slightly different product and advertising campaign. The business will select the key variables that differentiate the brands within a market.

A business can gain a competitive advantage in the market by reducing the price so it is less than their competitors'. However, there is a risk to this as the business could be offering products as a loss leader and not meet their production, marketing or finance costs. This would impact on the businesses long term profit. Although it could create a short term increase in sales. It could also lead to a price war within the market, with competitors also reducing their prices and trying to undercut the business and attract their customer base.

A business can add value to the product or service (giving a free toy to each sale). This strategy is used by McDonalds Happy meals and has been very successful. It makes customers believe that they are getting value for money on their purchase.

Another way to gain competitive advantage is through innovation, being able to quickly react to changing customers' needs and offering products or services that are at the front of the market. Innovation is a competitive strength especially within the technology market.

Competitive advantage is also gained through reliability offering a product or service that customers know or perceive that they can rely on. Quality when the product or service meets the customers' expectations and needs and is considered to be made to a good standard. Through reputation or image, advertising and branding, using the media effectively and being seen to have a positive presence. And lastly providing excellence in customer services, before, during and after the purchase. Customers will repeat buy and develop brand loyalty if they feel that the product is fit for purpose and offers them a positive experience.

Product differentiation is making a product or service different from other similar products in the market. So that customers will buy from the business because they want their product and not because it is the cheapest. This requires a fully integrated marketing programme, with set objectives that separate the business from its competitors. This can be achieved through displays, distribution channels and advertising.

Businesses can market themselves in a different way by having a unique selling point (USP). This will differentiate the product or services from competitors. A business can advise customers of the benefits of their products which saves customers time in selecting the best product to meet their needs and expectations. A UPS can be that products are better in some format such as quality or are cheaper than a competitors. Having a USP can allow businesses to gain competitive advantage and gain market share.

**Self-assessment questions**

1) Explain the methods used in conducting market research for business start-ups.
2) Describe the benefits and setbacks of research methods used for business start-ups.
3) Distinguish between qualitative and quantitative research. State three benefits of each.

**Activity 6:**

Log onto the internet and read the following article:

http://www.theguardian.com/small-business-network/2013/aug/23/small-business-tips-market-research

**Topic 1.2 - Market**

**Learning Outcome**

The aim of this section is for students to understand the following:

- Demand
- Supply
- Markets
- Price Elasticity of Demand
- Income Elasticity of Demand

**Demand**

**The Role of Demand in Markets**

Demand is a term that defines the number of products or services which customers are prepared to buy. With a limitless desire of wants and needs, demand identifies with the reality of the scarce nature of goods and services. Hence it focuses on the exact number of goods and services which will be sold instead of on perceived desires of the customers.

This is a more accurate measure of the demand for a product or service because the sales figures provide factual evidence of the customer behaviour towards the products. Furthermore, their willingness to pay for the product also helps reinforce the demand for the product.

When a product is in high demand, it could be limited in supply; however, as long as people are prepared to pay for the product, it would be available in the market, although in this case frequently at a premium price.

On the other hand, where there is a large number of products or services available which exceeds demand, these will be sold at a low price so that people can be attracted to buy the products.

**Activity 7 – What do you think is the relationship between demand and price of a product or service?**

## Relationship of demand and price

Price and Demand are inseparably linked for almost every product or service. With essential goods and services, the demand for these goods remains high despite the cost. These types of goods include basic items like water, groceries and other similar products. People need food to survive, and a scarcity of food does not deter people from buying it. Even when the price is high, it will be purchased (unless there are cheaper alternatives readily available).

Expensive products and services tend to have a lower demand. In order to make such products attractive and stimulate the demand for such, businesses make available various long-term payment plan options and also encourage the use of credit.

## Relationship of demand and competition

The greater the intensity of competition in a market; the greater the impact on price. Businesses innovate themselves in numerous ways to maintain high levels if demand and retain their customers. With tough competition, however, established businesses with trusted brands that consumers are loyal to still thrive well in such an environment. This is known as brand loyalty.

As long as customers trust a brand they will often be prepared to pay a higher price for it, as long as they remain satisfied with that product. Once the brand stops satisfying their needs, they will switch to another brand. The major reason for such a switch in brand loyalty is the price. Once there is a better value available, customers will go for it. Therefore competition between brands can affect demand.

Demand is also affected by close substitutes competing with each other for customers. Hence, when a customer moves between similar products to satisfy their need, then the demand is also affected.

**Relationship of consumer income and demand**

A consumer's disposable income will affect the demand for products and services. The higher a consumer's income, the greater will be the spending power of the consumer. However, when the income is lower, there will be a reduction in spending power. In effect, the amount a consumer is willing to spend on goods and services depends on their disposable income.

Net income is an individual's income after the deduction of tax. Generally, when the net incomes of customers fall, they tend to review and reduce their spending habits and prioritise what they need.

On the contrary, with high net incomes, consumers are willing to spend more and get more luxuries. In both cases, the demand is affected.

Every business must be aware of the need to advertise its existence and its products or services. Regardless of the high standard of quality of the goods, when the marketing strategy is poor, the product will remain unknown for a long period. During such a period, the demand will be relatively poor.

Seasonal fluctuations also can affect demand. Due to the nature of certain businesses, there are periods during the year which are busier than others. For example, during the summer months, there is an increase in demand for short-term holiday rentals by tourists and overseas visitors.

Apartment providers are very busy and try to meet the high volumes of demand. This does not mean that there are no bookings throughout the rest of the year; the demand is just higher in summer than at other times of the year.

Fashion, tastes and preferences can affect consumer demand, for example the latest iPhone. Customers will demand the latest fashionable products or services and will not want to have to wait for it. It is vital that a business is able to meet that demand in a timely manner and in the quantity required. Otherwise customers will look for the next best alternative, with a competitor.

Advertising and branding can have a huge impact on demand. It is a powerful tool that can make or break a business's success. Through having the correct advertising campaign a business can increase the demand for its products or services. Whilst advertising and branding can be expensive for a business it can pay off in increased sales, revenue and market share. Branding creates customer loyalty which creates demand for future purchases.

Demographics can affect demand for products which attract age groups: an older population may book more holidays on a cruise ship whereas a younger population may purchase more goods associated with technology mobile phones or computer games. Demographics are used in marketing planning and when considering launching new products. They will have little impact on a business operating on an international basis or online as they are able to access a wide and very large mass market. However, it will impact on small localised businesses whose target groups are in their geographical area.

External shocks can affect demand: for example war, terrorism, disease or health issues. These factors are unplanned and unpredictable but can have a major impact on demand. If one of these shocks occurs, it has a direct impact on businesses most affected such as airlines, travel companies and tourism. These businesses will attempt to maintain their level of demand, through price cuts.

## Supply

Supply is the amount that organisations can produce at a certain price; the amount a business produces is determined by price. The business will produce more if they anticipate higher profits. Changes in supply are determined by the cost of production which may increase the price to the consumer, and the business may sell fewer products. This reduction in sales will reduce organisations profits and will result in the organisation producing less.

Other influences on supply are new technology which may mean a reduction in costs, and the price to the customer will be reduced. An increase in indirect taxes, for example VAT, will increase prices and reduce the supply. Government subsidies in production will mean the cost of production will fall and this will lead to an increase in supply. External shocks, for example war, disease or weather extremes, will effect production of supply and lead to higher prices to the customer.

## Markets – Supply and Demand

The supply and demand of a product is determined by the interaction between consumers and the organisation that produce a product or provide a service. In an ideal world there should be economic equilibrium between demand and supply. If supply exceeds demand due to a high price for the product or services, there will be a surplus. If demand exceeds supply due to low prices, there will be a shortage of the product or service.

**Economic principles:**

- If there is a rise in demand (demand curve shifts to the right) and the supply remains the same this leads to a shortage and a higher equilibrium price
- If there is a fall in demand (demand curve shifts to the left) and supply remains the same this leads to a surplus and a lower equilibrium price
- If there is a rise in supply (supply curve shifts to the right) and demand remains the same this leads to a surplus and a lower equilibrium price
- If there is a fall in supply (supply curve shifts to the left) and demand remains the same this leads to a shortage and a higher equilibrium price

**Demand Curve**

This diagram shows a positive shift in demand that causes prices to rise and the quantity bought and sold to rise. Revenue expands from P1 and Q1 to P2 and Q2.

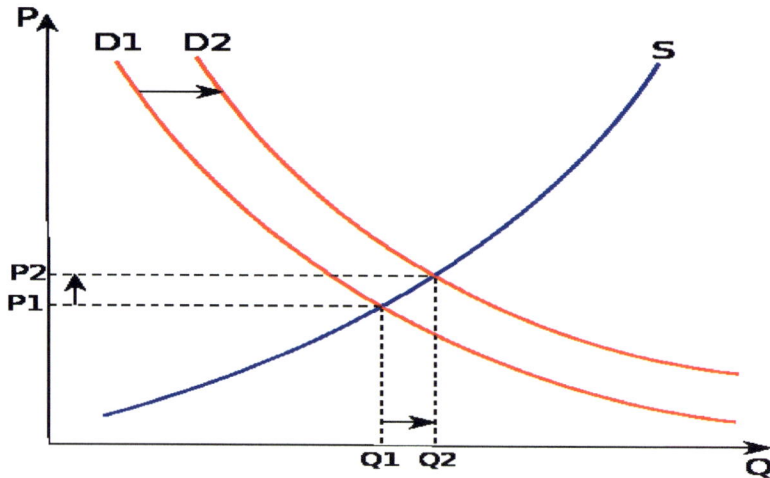

**Supply Curve**

This diagram shows a positive shift in supply which causes prices to fall from P1 to P2, resulting in the quantity bought and sold to rise from Q1 to Q2. Revenue changes from P1 and Q1 to P2 and Q2.

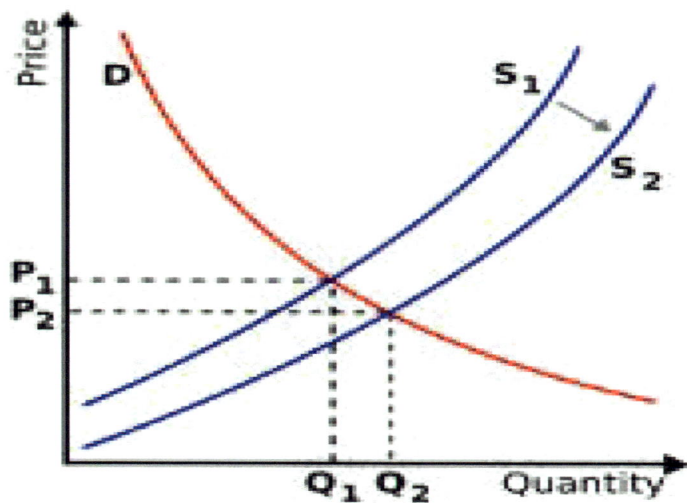

**Price Elasticity of Demand**

Price elasticity of demand is the measure of how the quantity of a product demanded would respond to the changes in its own price. When the demand is elastic, this means that a small change in the price could drastically affect the demand and lead to an enormous change in demand for that product (either positive or negative). Conversely, if the product is inelastic, then a large change in price will have little impact upon demand.

This is how it is calculated:

$$\text{PED} = \frac{\text{\% change in quantity demanded}}{\text{\% change in price}}$$

An example of this would be illustrated with two products that were independent of each other:

- Product x
- Product y

Let us say that both product x and y are sold at price £500 and the demand is 2000 units of each respective product. Now let us see what happens to the demand when the price of both products rises to £550.

Product x has a reduction in the quantity demanded from 2000 units to 1500 units. However, product y has a reduction in the quantity demanded from 2000 units to 1000 units. Based on this information, the price elasticity of demand (PED) can be calculated.

PED of product x  =  % change in quantity demanded

% change in price


PED  =  -25/10


PED  =  -2.5


PED of product y  =  % change in quantity demanded

% change in price


PED  =  -50/10


PED  =  -5.0


The result is always negative because the demand curve is a negative slope. However, when PED is calculated, it tends to be referred to in absolute terms without the negative sign.

When the change in quantity demanded is equal to the change in price, the elasticity of demand is in unity. This is termed unit price elasticity of demand.

The price elasticity of demand is affected by time, relative expense of the product and the attractiveness of a wide variety of substitutes available.

**Income Elasticity of Demand**

Income elasticity is a measure on how demand reacts to changes in income. With economic growth and the rise in the wealth of the nation, consumers tend to partake of this wealth as they see their incomes rising. Such income rises increase the demand for many products and services. Developed nations see the rise in demand for more durable products and services than for basic necessities like food. This is how it is calculated:

$$IED = \frac{\% \text{ change in quantity demanded}}{\% \text{ change in income}}$$

Positive income elasticity of demand occurs as the quantity demanded for products rise as the incomes of the consumer rises. Therefore the product is income-elastic. This tends to be the case for normal goods.

Negative income elasticity of demand occurs when the quantity demanded for products is less than the change in the income of the consumer. Low quality goods usually have negative elasticities because the more people earn, the greater the aspiration to keep up the lifestyle that comes with being rich.

When the change in quantity demanded is equal to the change in income, the elasticity of demand is unity. This is termed unit income elasticity of demand.

Cross-elasticity of demand is a measure of how the demand for a particular product reacts to the changes in price of another similar or related product.

$$XED = \frac{\% \text{ change in quantity demanded of product x}}{\% \text{ change in price of product y}}$$

Positive cross-elasticity of demand usually occurs with products which are close substitutes for each other. The rise in price of one product will see a sharp fall in its demand, and hence consumers will switch to its substitute which is more affordable and does the same work, if not even better – mobile phones are a good example of this.

Negative cross-elasticity of demand occurs when products complement each other. A price increase in one product will see the demand drop and will also see its complementary products experience a fall in demand.

**Relevance of price-elasticity of demand to total revenue of a firm**

The change in the total expenditure of consumers, as prices fluctuate can be explained by the price elasticity of demand. This acts on the assumption that the change in price is caused by a shift in the supply curve.

The total revenue of a firm or industry is based on the level of expenditure by consumers:

Total firm revenue = price x quantity = total consumer expenditure

When there is a change in the price of a product, consumers will react to such changes in various ways. Whatever reaction is taken by the consumer, it will affect their total expenditure and ultimately the revenue which the firm will generate.

**Topic 1.3 - Marketing Mix and Strategy**

**Learning Outcome**

The aim of this section is for students to understand the following:

- Product/service Design
- Branding and Promotion
- Pricing Strategies
- Distribution
- Marketing Strategy

**Product/Service Design**

The design of a product does not just concern its shape or appearance; it is much more than that. The function, durability and quality are a vital part and most be considered when the finished product is being designed. As customers are drawn to a product based on its appearance as much as its function.

**Design mix**

The design mix must consider three factors: aesthetics, function and cost.
Aesthetics looks at the appeal of the product to the senses, the look, taste, feel or smell. Perfume and fragrances are a prime example of the use of aesthetics as not only is the smell appealing, but the bottle and packaging that the perfume comes in is attractive.

The function of the product needs to be considered as the product needs to work, be durability and fit for purpose. Is the product strong enough or light enough for the customer's needs?

The cost is a consideration - is the design simple enough to be made efficiently and quickly?

Depending on the product all three elements of the mix may be of equal importance, although in most cases one of the factors will be the main focus.

**Changes in the elements of the design mix to reflect social trends**

Social trends, tastes and fashions are constantly changing and affect customer's needs and wants. It is vital that businesses stay ahead of these changes and remain innovative in order to remain competitive. By being flexible with the elements of the design mix they are able to prioritise the element that is most important and will allow the business to stay on trend.

**Concern over resource depletion, waste minimisation, re-use and recycle**

Businesses are concerned over the ability to continue to source raw materials or supplies. If they are reliant on natural resources they need to consider the fact that those supplies are finite in number and will become hard or impossible to obtain, at some point in the future.

It is in the businesses best interests to try to re-use and recycle as much as it possibly can. Not only will it meet its environmental or legal requirements but it may also save the business money. The same principle is applied to waste minimisation as business try to reduce their carbon footprint and also improve their manufacturing processes to reduce errors and therefore the amount of waste.

**Ethical sourcing**

Businesses seek to acquire raw materials and resources through sources that are ethical and sustainable. Such as the Body shop or the Co-op bank.

Ethical sourcing can allow a business to have an USP especially if competitors have not embraced this ideology. This may give a business a competitive advantage.

Consumers are much more concerned with the impact that the products or services that they are buying have on their place of origin and the impact that the provision of this product or service may have on people and places.

For example: Fair trade was set up to protect producers of coffee or cocoa beans and ensure that they receive a fair price for their raw materials. Consumers feel that they are contributing to a fair and equal system and that the products are ethical sourced.

**The Purpose of Marketing**

Marketing is defined as the process of identification, anticipation and satisfaction of customer expectations and needs. To achieve these goals, a business must view itself from the perspective of its customers. The marketing mix is used by the business to realise its marketing targets. The marketing mix utilises the combination of four vital elements to implement its marketing strategy. Effective marketing uses a range of strategies from:

- Communication
- Pricing decisions
- New product development
- Research

Marketing can be categorised under:

- Business-to-business
- Consumer marketing

Both types of marketing use different tools to advance their products, including:

| Advertising | Corporate hospitality |
|---|---|
| Discounting | Face-to-face sales |
| Customer loyalty schemes | Point-of-sale materials |
| Direct mail | Publicity |

**Branding and Promotion**

**Niche and Mass Marketing**

Niche marketing focuses on a small sector of a larger market. By producing and providing specific products to satisfy the needs of this niche segment, the business can profit from a market where there is little competition and potentially high margins.

For this reason, the output of the business does cover the overheads of the business. In effect, success in this market means that the products have high prices which help to offset the fixed costs per unit of the business.

Mass marketing focuses on a low prices and high volume of sales to as wide an audience as possible.

By provision of products to suit the needs of the whole market these products become brand names. It has been used by many superior household names such as Procter and Gamble, Nestle, Coca-Cola and many more.

**Activity 8 – Can you think of any niche market companies or products?**

**Designing an Effective Marketing Mix**

The marketing mix is used by the business to realise its marketing targets. The marketing mix utilises the combination of four vital elements to implement its marketing strategy. These factors are:

- Price
- Place
- Promotion
- Product

The marketing mix is influenced by:

Finance - This is used to develop new ideas. Sometimes these may fail at the early stages. However, after several stages and planning, implementation and testing, products are finally deemed satisfactory for the market.

Technology – This is used to provide the widest possibility of options to the business in how it markets its product. The greater the use of technology, the more successful the strategy of marketing will be. From Digital advertising to the use of internet and television amongst other forms of media advertising, technology is a major force that can produce tremendous results.

Market research - This provides the opportunity for the business to correctly identify the consumer needs and exploit the opportunities for development of new trends. Through market research, effective ways of reaching the target market and identifying vital characteristics of the market can be identified.

The market mix used depends on the type of market and what works best. When a market mix is integrated it takes into consideration the sales, product and production orientation. Furthermore, the orientation of the market is also explored.

**The Product Marketing Mix – USPs, Product Portfolio Analysis and Product Lifecycle**

The process of product development enables a business to establish a range of products and services which it offers to the market. There are different stages in product development, and the business needs to see this as a profitable investment.

- Creativity
- Defining the concept
- Developing the concept
- Testing and finalising the concept
- Product Launch
- Lifecycle management

The managerial skill of the organisations leadership is important in influencing the process of product development. Furthermore, the level of competition in the market influences the development process. Technology also determines product development.

Through the revolution that is the Internet, some businesses that had previously been into traditional methods of marketing and retailing their products have now become heavily involved in the use of available technology advancements, often to their benefit.

**Unique Selling Point (USP)**

Unique Selling Points (USP) are distinct features of a product or service that gives it an edge and makes it stand out from other products in the market; they are things that make your product different from the others in the same niche. Through unique selling points, consumers are able to differentiate products. A USP needs to be attractive and strong enough to expand the number of new customers which the business has.

**Product portfolio analysis**

This analysis is based on three different matrices which are as follows:

Ansoff Matrix - This considers the marketing concepts through the product development, market penetration, diversification and market development. It focuses on the future prospects of the business and how to achieve such plans through marketing of its products and services.

The Boston Growth Matrix - This is based on the concept of the product lifecycle. This lifecycle identifies the opportunities of introduction, growth, maturity and decline. It was developed to analyse businesses and products through its growth in the market and its share of the market. It uses the cash cow, wild cat, dog and star terms to refer to various aspects of the business and its performance in terms of market share and its market growth.

General Electric Screen Matrix - This is used to cross-reference the attractiveness of the business and considers the variables which relate to the actual market. These include:

- Size of the market
- Size of competitors
- Market growth rate
- Number of competitors
- Technological implications
- Potential entry barriers
- Profit margins

**Activity 9 – What is a USP? Identify some products which have one.**

**Product lifecycle**

All products go through phases from when they are created to when they are withdrawn from the market. The product lifecycle is the process that describes these phases starting from its introduction into the market through to its final removal from the market. These stages include the following:

- Introduction
- Growth
- Maturity
- Decline

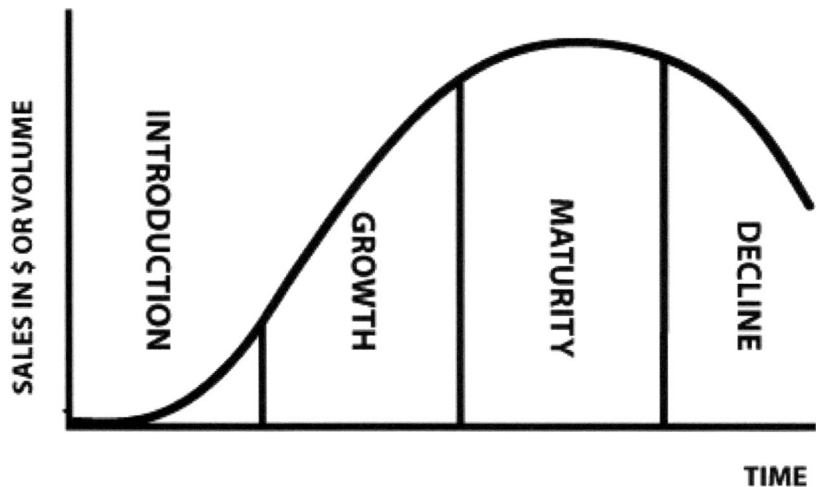

The more successful a product is in the market, the more competitors will strive to replicate such products. This could lead to the market overflow of such a product.

Ultimately, this can impact on older products which could be forced out of the market. The business must then decide whether or not to discontinue such a product or let it just phase out of the market.

Rink and Swan (1979) demonstrated the product lifecycle management with the use of various patterns of the lifecycle from:

| Classical | Cycle-recycle |
|---|---|
| Cycle-half recycle | Increasing/decreasing |
| High/low plateau | Stable maturity |
| Growth maturity | Innovative maturity |
| Growth decline plateau | Rapid penetration |

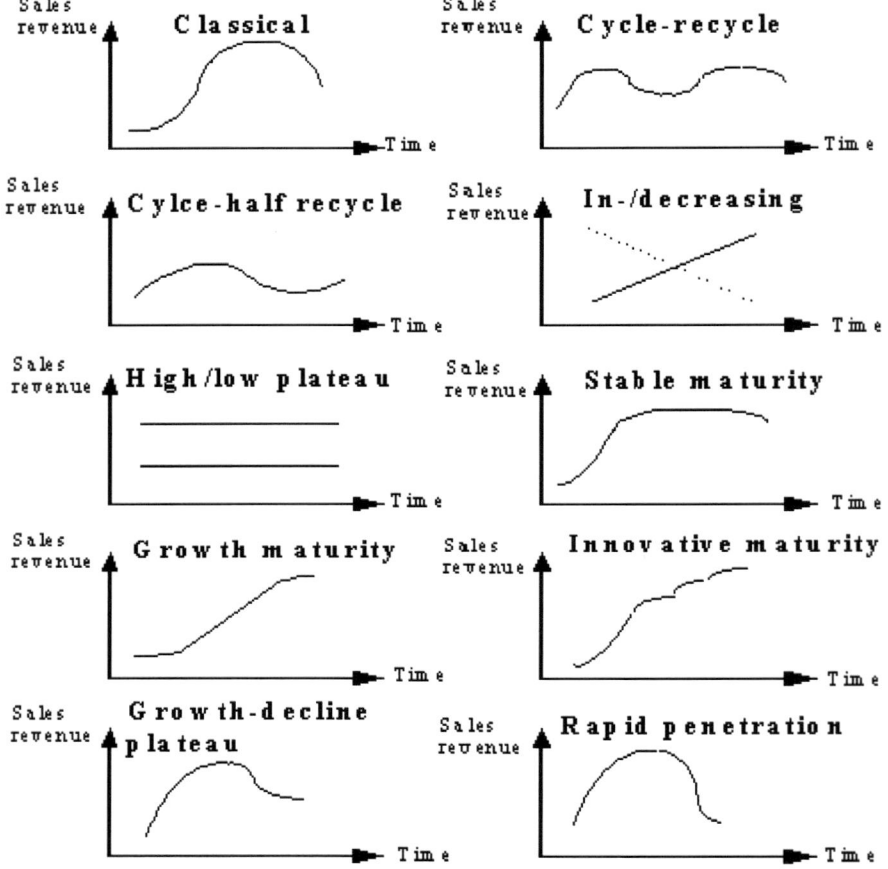

Extension strategies are used by the business to maintain a high volume of sales throughout the product life especially as the product reaches its maturity stage. It uses promotion and advertising strategies to avoid the product decline stage.

78

**The Promotion Marketing Mix: Above-the-Line, Below-the-Line**

The process of marketing a product is, to a large degree, dependent on communication. Through communication, information about the product is relayed to the consumer. A business must use the most effective method to communicate with its customers.

Promotion marketing mix could be:

- Above-the-line - Above-the-line refers to the use of the services of advertising agencies to market the products and services of the business. These include the use of mobile advertising, press advertising, cinema advertising, internet advertising, radio advertising, posters and billboards. Advertising is the use of public, paid and non-sponsored announcements of a message which is intended to persuade a target audience by a sponsor who is identified. It is an integral component in marketing of products and services to customers. Above-the-line the line promotional mix uses push and pull strategies which intend to distribute and advertise simultaneously

- Below-the-line - Below-the-line advertising refers to the use of activities including merchandising, branding direct mail, point-of-sale, public relations and direct selling. Public relations aims to establish and maintain goodwill, deal promptly with unfavourable publicity, establish and maintain prestige and reputation of the business. The promotional marketing mix refers to the use of two or more elements which may include personal selling, sales promotion, advertising and public relations. Several other influences on the promotional marketing mix include corporate image, sponsorship, exhibitions, customer service, internet/email, internal marketing and word of mouth. A promotional budget is the amount of financial resources that are allocated by a business to promotions over a period of time

**Pricing Strategies**

**The Pricing Marketing Mix – Pricing Strategies, Price Tactics**

Price is one of the four original Ps of the marketing mix. It is essentially the amount a customer is willing to pay for your product. It can be categorised into three areas:

- Competition – from lower-priced market segments; direct competitors
- Cost – these include variable costs
- Customer – perceptions of quality and price expectations, previous prices

Pricing strategies include market skimming, product mix, cost plus, market penetration pricing, discriminatory, product bundle and psychological amongst others. Pricing strategies also include the use of:

- Penetration pricing
- Predatory pricing
- Price skimming
- Price leaders and takers

Price tactics are another form of strategising through the use of price. They are used short-term and have a maximum effect. Due to its very nature, it can be changed or abandoned as the circumstances change. These tactics include:

| Prestige pricing | Price bundling |
|---|---|
| Loss leaders | Off-peak pricing |
| Competitive pricing | Differential pricing |
| Cost-plus pricing | Odd-even pricing |

Several influences that affect decisions on pricing include the price elasticity of demand, price sensitivity and non-price competition.

## The Place Marketing Mix – Outlets and Distributors Choices, Distribution Channels

The marketing mix is not complete without considering the location of the business.

Businesses that strive for improved success levels are aware of the implications of the product and services reaching customers in a timely manner. A number of considerations include:

- Persuasion of other businesses to increase stock of their products
- Transportation of goods and services from factories and outlets, importers and suppliers to the final end user – the consumer

Distribution is the physical movement of products or services from the producer to the end-user. It involves ownership transfer of the products or services through the use of intermediaries between producers and the consumer – the final end-user.

The channel of distribution utilises transport and storage companies as well as banks. Several types of distribution include:

- Indirect distribution
- Multiple distribution
- Direct distribution
- Distribution research

Three major channels of distribution include traditional, direct and modern distribution channels. Popular forms of distribution are performed by the use of agents, retailers, wholesalers and the choice of the right channel.

**Self-assessment questions**

1) Explain the importance of effective Marketing.

2) Describe the process of designing an effective marketing mix.

3) What are the four components of the marketing mix?

**Marketing Strategy**

**Understanding Marketing Objectives**

Marketing objectives are the goals and aims which a business strives to achieve through the process of marketing its products.

It involves a planning process that revolves around the following:

- Corporate objectives
- Marketing objectives
- Marketing analysis
- Marketing strategies
- Marketing plans

They usually tend to include targeting of new segments of a market, the development of new goods and services and maintaining or increasing the market share.

**Activity 10 – What do you think the objective of a marketing campaign is?**

Below is a diagram showing the influences on the marketing objectives:

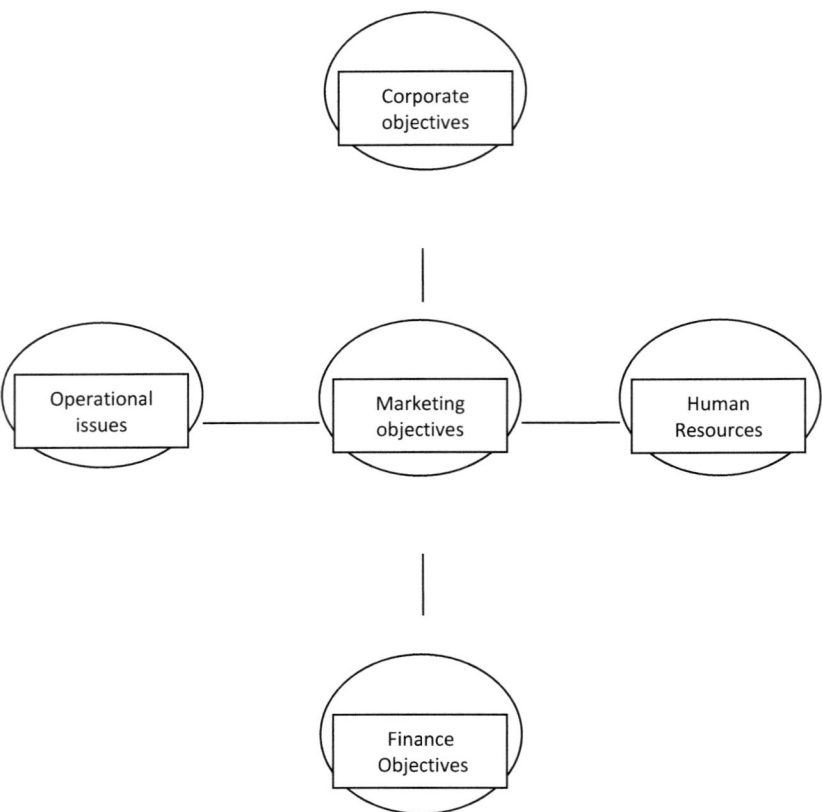

The effective combination of these internal factors have strong outcome on the ability of the business to have a strong marketing objective.

Below are the external factors which affect the marketing objective. The effective combination of these external factors have a strong outcome on the ability of the business to have a strong marketing objective.

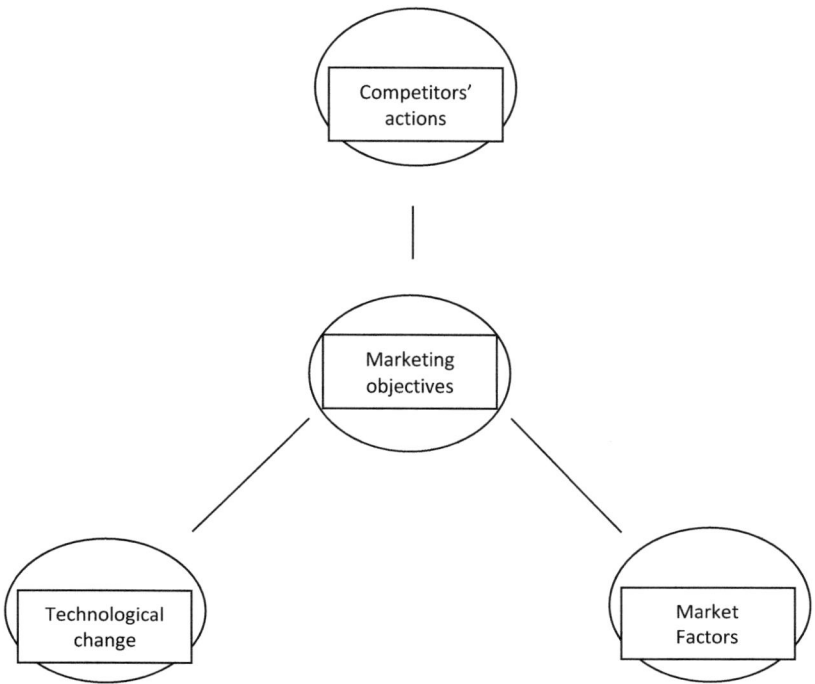

**Analysing Markets and Marketing**

The importance of analysing a market provides the basis for a business to identify sales patterns and devising unique strategies to target the market.

It involves the use of several methods which include:

- Extrapolation
- Correlation
- Moving average

Thorough market analysis provides an insight into the trends of the market, competitive behaviour and ways of reinforcing the competitiveness of the business.

Analysing market data can be difficult because of the amount of information and resource involved. Furthermore, the analysis has to be as accurate as possible if it is to have any value.

The rise of information technology has changed the way we analyse markets. More data can be analyses simultaneously and with greater accuracy.

It is also beneficial because it can be used to build up an electronic database of consumer behaviour in terms of buying or likes. Furthermore, it enables the business to customise its ability to target the market and customers based on the profile information which it possesses of client behaviour.

## Selecting Marketing Strategies

A business implements the strategies it believes will achieve its marketing ambitions for the products and services. These strategies enable the business to optimise its potential for its products or services. The strategies of a business must be tailored to suit the market that the organisation operates in. The decision to use the strategy of differentiation, or low cost marketing, is very important. Whether in mass or niche markets, low cost options can be viable depending on the circumstance. Furthermore, the strategy of differentiation is also used to make products look different in terms of its superiority in comparison to other products as well as to show its uniqueness.

The Ansoff Matrix considers the marketing concepts through the product development, market penetration, diversification and market development. It focuses on the future prospects of the business and how to achieve such plans through marketing of its products and services.

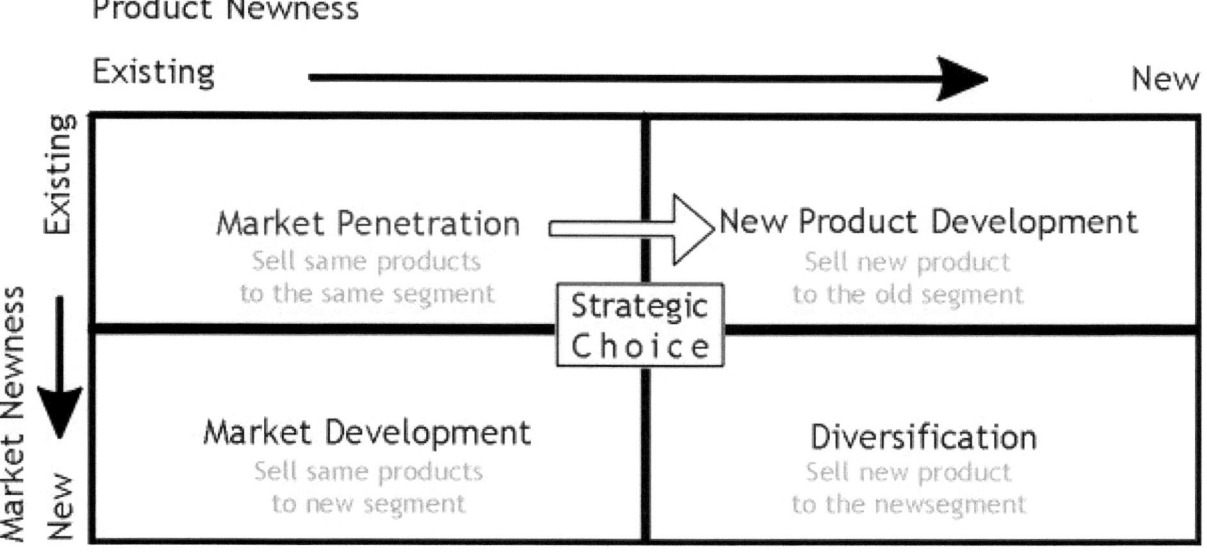

Market penetration is a strategy which is used to increase current sales of products to both new customers and existing customers.

Product development is used to create new products for the market through innovation and development.

Market development on the other hand is used to attract new customers to existing products. Diversification involves the use of unique strategies to venture into new markets which are not related to its current range of products and services.

When a business considers entering an international market it needs to explore opportunities for such entries and the benefits of the potential markets, weighed against the drawbacks of the market.

**Developing and Implementing Marketing Plans**

A market plan is used to formulate the specific actions which need to be taken by a business to optimise the effect of its products and services on the market. It sets a target time frame, describes the elements of the marketing mix and justifies the reasons for each action that it takes. The components of a marketing plan include:

- SWOT Analysis
- Marketing objectives
- Budgets
- Sales forecasts
- Marketing strategies
- Situation analysis

This is shown diagrammatically:

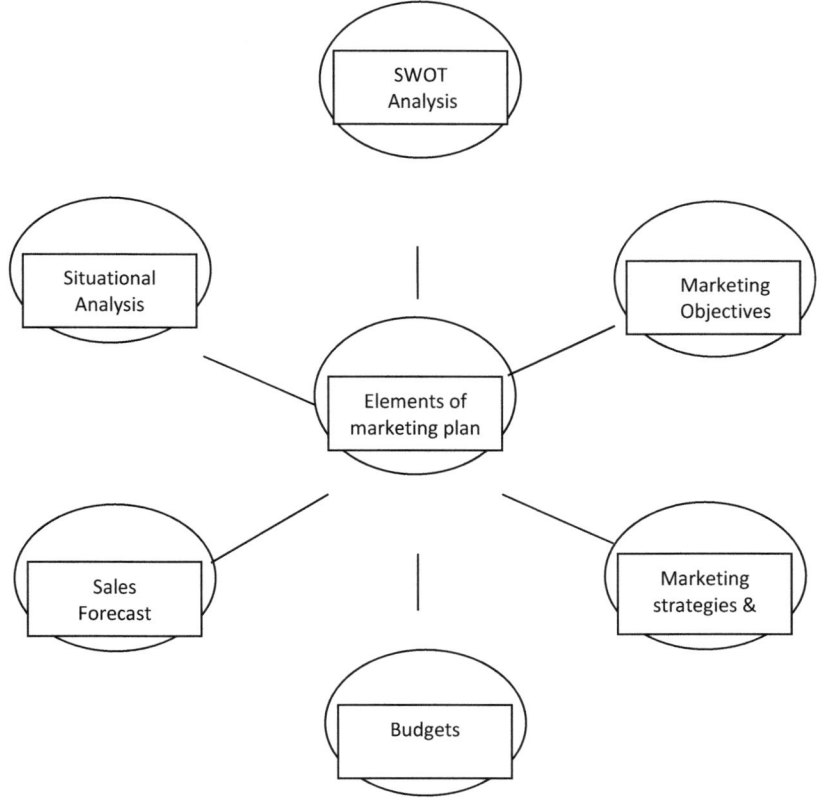

The effective combination of these above factors formulates a practical plan of marketing.

There are internal influences on marketing plans:

- Operational issues
- Availability of finance
- Human resources

There are external influences on marketing plans:

- Market conditions
- Actions of market competitors
- Changes in technology

Issues involved in the implementation of market plans involve the resources required. Furthermore, the key tasks involved in such plans of marketing must be effectively scheduled. Due control of the market plan needs to be established. It is also important to realise the need to add the cost of the marketing plan in the budget.

**Activity 11 – What is a SWOT analysis?**

**Boston Matrix**

This matrix has been developed to assist organisations to analyse their product lines, allocate resources correctly and to use the matrix as an analytical tool in brand marketing. It analyses the market share of each of the businesses products and the rate of growth of the markets in which they operate.

| BCG-Matrix | | relatief marktaandeel | |
| --- | --- | --- | --- |
| | | hoog | laag |
| groeipotentieel | hoog | star | question mark |
| | laag | cash cow | dog |

Product or service lines are plotted on the matrix next to the relevant sections. It can allow a business to make decisions to withdraw products that are no longer profitable.

CASH COW

A cash cow is where a business has a high market share but with little growth. These product lines or services should be 'milked' with little investment required. An example of a cash cow would be Kellogg's Corn Flakes or Coca Cola.

DOGS

A dog is a product or service line in a slow-to-mature industry. This line typically breaks even and does not generate high levels of profit. For example, DVD recorders have made video records obsolete in the technology market.

STARS

A star is a product or service in a high market share with high growth such high fashion products or PlayStation in the games market.

QUESTION MARKS

These products or service have low market share in a growth market and may become the next star. The cost of developing this product will be more than the return in the early product lifecycle. These are often the starting point for a new business and must be watched carefully such as a new car model or the development of a new computer game.

In general, a business needs to keep a cash cow, sell off dog products or services, retain star products and invest in question marks.

**Self-assessment questions**

- Explain the importance of effective Marketing.
- Describe the process of designing an effective marketing mix.
- What are the four components of the marketing mix?

**Self-assessment questions**

- Define a business marketing strategies.
- Explain the importance of marketing objectives in a business.
- Outline the process of analysing markets and marketing.
- Highlight four ways of selecting marketing strategies.
- What are the processes of developing and implementing marketing plans?

**Activity 12 - Log on the internet and read the following articles:**

http://www.independent.co.uk/news/business/news/facebook-revenue-up-63-per-cent-thanks-to-massive-increase-in-mobile-advertising

http://www.independent.co.uk/news/business/news/bt-boss-blasts-labour-for-negative-stance-over-business-ads

**Topic 1.4 - Managing People**

**Learning Outcome**

The aim of this section is for students to understand the following:

- Approaches to Staffing
- Recruitment, Selection and Training
- Organisational Design
- Motivation Theory and Practice
- Leadership

**Approaches to Staffing**

**Workforce Roles**

The role of the workforce is carried out by the various employees, at all different levels, who occupy jobs in the organisations.

The directors are often the owners of the company and at the very least tend to have some financial stake in the company.

Every business that is at least medium sized will have managers at different levels within the business. The roles they play within the organisation will depend upon their level of seniority and what they are responsible for.

The responsibilities of managers will generally include ensuring employees perform their assigned tasks efficiently.

Managers will provide the resources for the job to be done and monitor performance of employees on their tasks to ensure it is in accordance with the desired performance level.

The team leader takes control of a team of workers to facilitate success of the team in accomplishing tasks. Their objectives include assisting team members in development efforts, creating an atmosphere for the free flow of information and the exchange of ideas, and implementing business improvements.

Supervisors are at the lower tier of the management and make up the first line of management responsible for work groups. They guide and direct the workers in the performance of work tasks to a satisfactory standard.

**Delegation and Communication Flows, Job Allocation and Workloads**

**Delegation**

Delegation is an important skill for all managers to develop. It enables a manager or the leader of a team to assign specific responsibilities to subordinates. Those subordinates must also be given the authority to execute the responsibilities allocated to them. There needs to be:

- Clear definition of the tasks
- Strong authority of the leader who delegates the task to the subordinate
- Informing colleagues of the specific subordinate authority and responsibility of the subordinate

Limitations of delegation include:

- Sometimes costly as you need to train the person you are delegating to
- Over-delegation or under-delegation can lead to serious difficulties. It needs to be balanced
- The need to understand that not all tasks can actually be delegated

**Flow of communication**

Communication needs to flow within an organisation freely and efficiently. With greater levels of hierarchy, the more difficult the communication of information becomes. Managers must always be considering the most effective ways to communicate messages and instructions; this is becoming even more significant with the development of mass communication technologies.

**Job allocation and workloads**

A business can improve its levels of efficiency by assigning specific responsibilities for particular jobs to individuals, teams, sections or departments.

There is the need to spread the load of work evenly in an organisational structure.

Where it is necessary, additional workers need to be employed in areas which directly enhance the level of sales revenue.

Alternatively moving staff from one department to another, to spread the workload evenly, can be employed. However, this can cause problems with staff resentment.

It needs to be noted that the range of responsibilities which get allocated to any specific job role will have its effects on the amount of workload involved.

**Activity 13 – What do you think could be the effect upon a business of poor communications?**

**Flexible Workforce**

Employees who are flexible are multi-skilled and will complete a range of different tasks in the business. They have a wide range of skills and the ability to change between roles flawlessly. These members of staff are an asset to the business as it means that they offer the business flexibility and also reduce the need for staff to remain fixed in one role. There is a cost involved in training staff to this level, but ultimately it will benefit the business.

These employees may have a number of different types of employment contracts:

- Full-time or part-time
- Zero hours contract (no set hours per week)
- Relief contract (as and when required)
- Seasonal (required during busy periods for example the school holidays)
- Temporary or permanent
- Flexi-time or shift work

The advantages of flexible working for the employer are that they can employ staff as and when they need them, such as if production increases and staff can complete a number of roles so the employer does not need to increase total workforce numbers. The advantages for the employee are that the work is varied completing different tasks and helps prevent boredom.

The disadvantage for the employer are that if staff do not have permanent hours, they may look for employment elsewhere meaning retention of skilled employees could be a problem. For the employee they may not have guaranteed hours each week, and shift work (unsociable hours) may not suit their personal circumstances.

**Dismissal and Redundancy**

Dismissal is when an employee is fired or sacked from their job, which may be due to a disciplinary issue in the workplace. There is a set sequence of steps involved in this process, unless the issue is serious enough to require instant dismissal, such as an assault. Redundancy is when the business is reducing the size of the workforce; in some circumstances redundancy can be voluntary.

**Employer and Employee Relationships**

An individual employee can communicate with the employer to negotiate their employment contract, working conditions and rate of pay. Workforce representatives either as a group or through a Trade Union (for example UNISON) may communicate with management; this is known as collective bargaining. Trade unions represent their members to improve economic and working conditions in the workplace.

**Self-assessment questions**

- What are functions of people in business?
- Describe the key elements of organisational structure.
- Discuss the importance of delegation and communication flows, job allocation and workloads.

**Recruitment selection and training**

**The Process of Recruitment**

Selecting the right people to work for you is of fundamental importance to the success of your business. There are several processes involved in this:

- The selection process - The selection process involves the steps taken by the business from the identification of the need to filling the vacancy. A job description should specify the roles and responsibilities and the skills required
- Application forms - Application forms are used by many businesses to allow applicants to express their interest in the job. With companies that require application forms they usually ask for a covering letter also. The trend for using application forms is declining in favour of CVs
- Curriculum Vitae (CVs) - CVs are frequently used by businesses instead of standard applications. The CV summarises the educational, work and extra-curricular activities and experiences of the candidate which are relevant to the job description
- Assessing applications - Assessing applications are done by the business after a satisfactory number of qualified candidates have responded to the job advertised or after the closing date for applications. There is usually a deadline in which the applications are accepted, after which the assessment begins. Businesses look for accuracy and consistency in information provided, the candidate's skills and capabilities, and their relevance to the job

**Internal and External Recruitment**

**Internal recruitment**

Internal recruitment is the process by which you fill an available vacancy with an employee who currently works for the business. This is often called promotion from within.

By so doing, a business recognises that it has existing employees that can satisfy the vacancy to a satisfactory standard, without having to look for candidates outside of the organisation.

Advantages of internal recruitment:

- Recruiters have a strong knowledge of capabilities of applicant
- It is quicker than external recruitment
- The employees enjoy opportunities for career projection and development
- It encourages employees to be retained and advance in the business

Disadvantages include:

- Lack of fresh ideas by new entrants to the business which could lead to stagnation
- The idea of an internal vacancy implies that once it has been filled, a vacant position is automatically created
- It limits the candidates for the job exclusively to employees who may not necessarily be best suited for the new role

**External recruitment**

For most businesses this is the most common form of recruitment.

With this method, available vacancies are filled by people from outside of the organisation.

It can also employ the specialist skills of agencies that screen candidates and short-list the best candidates for the interview process.

Organisations can also employ the media in raising awareness of the vacant roles, thereby attracting a broad pool of candidates.

External recruitment can be time-consuming and expensive. There are advertising costs, recruitment agency costs (often a one-off fee of 40% of the salary of the individual) etc. Typically anyone you hire who is currently employed by another company, will require a notice period, frequently at least 4 weeks for a managerial level appointment.

**Activity 14 – Outline the advantages and disadvantages of internal and external recruitment.**

**How to Choose the Best Employee**

Selecting the correct employees is vital for the success of a business. There will almost certainly be numerous applicants for every vacancy, and choosing the right one from a vast array of information is incredibly difficult.

Based on information provided by the applicant, the process of assessment will thoroughly scrutinise the applicants' details, and eliminate any candidates whose answers are inconsistent or incomplete. There is often a tendency for candidates to exaggerate and falsify information, and failure by the prospective employer to confirm information provided can prove to be a major complication at a later stage. For instance, it could lead to hiring an unqualified or unsuitable candidate.

Interviews are an important stage of the selection process. Both face-to-face interviews and telephone interviews are very popular. Face-to-face interviews could be:

- Panel interviews
- Serial interviews
- Group interviews
- One-on-one interviews
- Sequential interviews

The use of tests is also becoming common. These are usually of two types:

- Psychometric tests
- Personality questionnaires

These can provide an insight into the competencies, actions and attitudes of candidates in very situations. These provide a form of assessment of the behaviour of the candidate; however, these tests are not universally accepted as sound.

**Workforce Improvement through Recruitment and Selection**

Your workforce should always have the interests of the business as a whole at the heart of what they do. In some cases the workforce can be described as the work family, and everyone should ensure that they are both working to the best of their ability, and that they are working safely.

Based on this, it is important that the recruitment and selection of candidates will continue to hire the best individual with a strong work ethos and commitment to the business. This has several implications:

- Creating an atmosphere of hard work and determination to excel. New employees should make effort to display this attribute
- Increased levels of support offered by managers and leaders of teams
- New external employees create fresh ideas and enhance the business chances of sustaining competitiveness
- Internal employees are motivated to perform and stay within the business when there are opportunities for internal progression
- Businesses which create better conditions for work and work flexibility tend to see the employees willing to perform better

**Activity 15 – What do you think will be the effect on the business of hiring the wrong kind of employees?**

**Methods of Training**

Several methods of training can be used to develop the skills of the workforce:

- Induction - The induction process involves welcoming the newly-recruited members of staff to the company. It also involves guided tours of the organisation, familiarisation with the work environment, accompanied introductions to other team members, to mention a few. The induction can be up to several weeks or a full day and can include information on holiday entitlement, working patterns, expenses, health and safety, training and development etc.
- Staff development - Staff development is used to assist the staff in pursuing further development and enhancement opportunities. It is a vital form of business investment in its manpower
- In-house training - In-house training utilises customised training especially designed for the business. This is usually provided by project leaders, external specialists, human resources and supervisors and management
- On-the-job training - On-the-job training is done in the actual work environment of the employee. This could be done through mentoring by experienced employees, coaching processes and shadowing experienced employees and supervisors, managers or team leaders
- External training - External training involves training on sales and customer services, management and Health and Safety. It involves attending courses in colleges and institutions outside the work environment. These tend to be based around knowledge, specific skills and abilities of the employee and not on the organisation

**Self-assessment questions**

- Discuss the ways through which a business can develop an effective workforce.
- Describe the process of recruitment in a business enterprise.
- What are the benefits and drawbacks of internal and external recruitment?
- What are the methods of workforce improvement through recruitment and selection?

**Organisational Design**

**Elements of Organisational Structure – Hierarchy and Spans of Control**

Organisational structure is traditionally represented as a form of a family tree. Its purpose is to show the interrelationships between people and departments, as well as their relative superiority within the organisation.

The organisational structure depicts the structure of the different departments, levels of responsibility of the members of staff, like the managers and supervisors. It also shows the communication lines and how information is passed around the business. Here is an example:

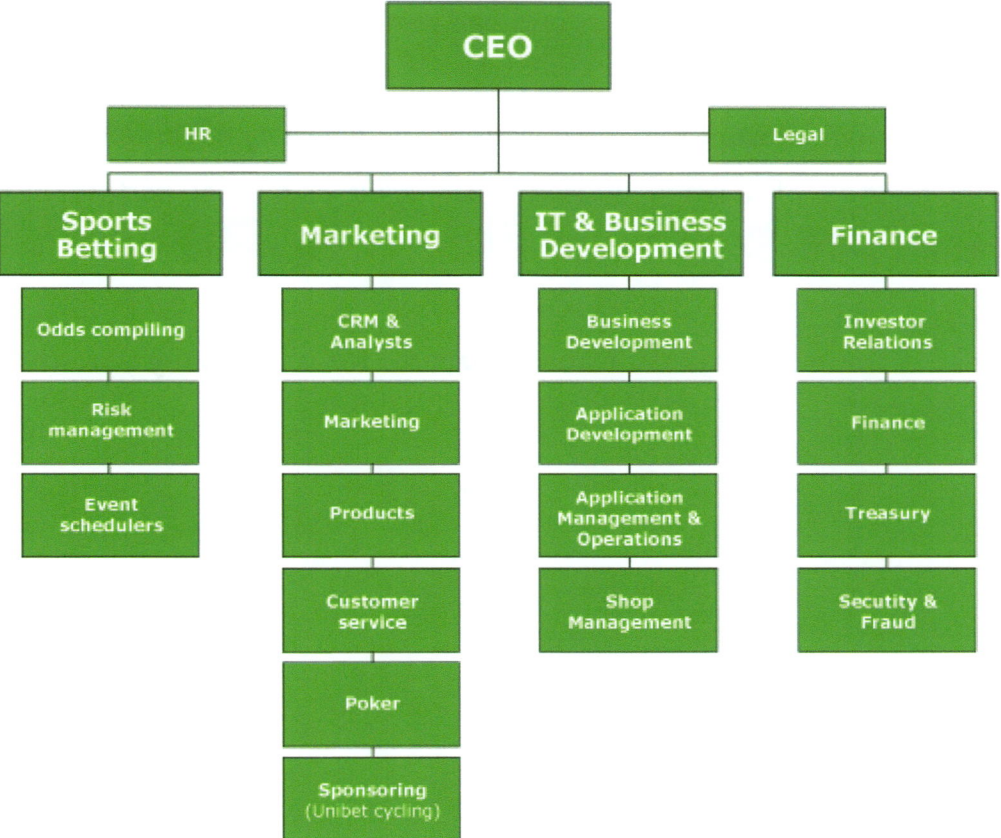

Charts illustrate in a graphical manner the organisation of the business in a clear, concise and easy-to-understand manner.

There are organisation trees that are similar in function to the chart and provide diagrammatic representation of the business.

There are also other elements in the structure of the organisation. These include:

- Hierarchies
- Spans of control
- Layers of management

Organisational structures show hierarchies in the business, and the different departments within the business. It can be beneficial and detrimental to the business because a structure that is too hierarchical can be rigid and inflexible.

Spans of control show the manager's line of control and responsibilities for the team or department. It is essential to know what a manager can reasonably handle efficiently in order to prevent undue difficulties and bad performance of leaders.

Layers of management show that organisations could be very flat or tall in its structure. Whichever method of layering is used must result in greater performance of the personnel.

**Activity 16 – Draw an organisational structure for a company you are familiar with.**

Some organisations have a centralised management structure where they have one person or headquarters to make decisions and provide direction for the business as a whole, across all of its locations. Small business often operates this way with the owner being the main decision maker. A decentralised organisation has several individuals who are responsible for making decisions and running the business.

The advantage of a centralised organisation is that decision-making is carried out by senior management, and it is easier to implement common policies across the organisation. The disadvantages are that a centralised structure can be bureaucratic with many layers of hierarchy, which results in slow decision making. A centralised organisation may also make decisions that are not suitable for all of its locations, and not take into account local customs or practices.

The advantages of decentralisation are that decision-making is closer to the customer which improves customer service. This also means the organisation can respond quicker to local circumstances. The disadvantages are that the organisation may find it difficult to have control of consistent policies. They may also find that decision-making may not follow the strategic aims of the organisation.

**Motivation**

**Financial Methods of Motivation**

Businesses use several methods of motivating employees, including:

- Commissions - Commission is a fraction of the total sales value earned by the worker. Tips for people who work in the restaurant sector can have a similar effect

- Bonuses - Bonuses are rewards to high-performing employees, and the business overall, for the achievement of defined targets and goals. These are paid at a particular time of the year in one lump sum

- Performance related pay – This can be given to high performers in a particular company. They can also be awarded through individual appraisals

- Job satisfaction - This involves a continuous drive to motivate the workers so that they can have satisfactory levels of performance. This implies that there must be a very high degree of pleasure and enjoyment which the employees expect to derive from work

- Fringe benefits - These are known as the non-financial rewards employees receive. They can include gym memberships, discounts on company products, company cars, private health care etc. Innovative companies are constantly looking to improve their fringe benefits as they can have a significant impact on performance and morale, and are usually cheaper than a direct pay rise

- Pensions - Non-contributory pensions are made by the employer on behalf of the employee. Contributory pensions are made by both the employer and employee into a pension scheme. Final salary pensions are often considered the best, but these are now few and far between for new employees

- Piece work – This is getting paid for each piece that you make. Therefore, the more you make the more that you earn

**Improvement of Job Design**

Job design ensures that the responsibilities and tasks of the employee are challenging and interesting.

When jobs are tedious and repetitive, employees can become very demotivated. Safety can become an issue as concentration lapses; quality can also suffer. Jobs should be designed to keep employees stimulated.

It is influenced by several factors:

- Variety of skills
- Significance of task
- Task identity
- Autonomy
- Feedback

These factors affect the other components of job design which determine the attractiveness of the job in terms of what it has to offer to the employee designated to do the job. These components include:

- Job enrichment
- Job rotation
- Job enlargement

The greater these components, the stronger the motivation will be for the workforce to perform to excellent standards.

**Employee Empowerment**

Empowerment provides employees with the opportunities of actively participating in the decision-making processes of the business. Employees often need to have the satisfaction of knowing that their opinions and views are valued by their employer.

There are a number of types of empowerment: including:

- Delegation
- Job enrichment
- Self-management

Employee empowerment is not a new concept. Although there is no clearly established link between empowerment and performance, it is widely believed that there is some level of correlation between the two.

In order to correctly utilise empowerment, the employees need to be trained, supported and provided with access to sufficient tools for information.

Trust must be established between the management and employees in order for empowerment to work.

A manager can impart trust through support and training and provision of ample learning opportunities for the employees.

Line managers also need to listen to, and act upon, suggestions by the work force; if they do not, then the workforce will quickly lose motivation and they will not feel part of a wider company-wide team.

**Team Working**

The ability to work in teams is very important to most businesses. When used well, it provides the platform for successful attainment of individual and business goals.

Teams are known to develop productivity and increase the quality of the work. Furthermore, the levels of customer satisfaction are improved. Through teamwork, wastage is reduced and there is improvement in job satisfaction.

Team functions can be categorised in to three groups:

- Tasks to achieve team objective and goal
- Interaction among the team to accomplish set tasks
- Self-focusing on individual responsibilities to the team and performing them optimally to achieve team goals

Team roles can be function-based or task-based. Function-based roles involve embarking upon tasks to facilitate the job. These include expressers, gate-keepers, harmonisers, encouragers and compromisers.

Task-based team roles involve the roles that actually get the job done. These include information seekers, agreement testers, initiators, summarisers and elaborators.

**Activity 18 – Is teamwork always the best thing for businesses and employees?**

**Motivation Theories**

Motivation of employees is a constant issue that any manager and business owner needs to consider. There have been different theories of motivation by several individuals. Authors of these theories include:

- Douglas McGregor
- FW Taylor
- Abraham Maslow
- Frederick Hertzberg
- Elton Mayo

Douglas McGregor's theory of motivation identified the theory X and theory Y concept of motivation.

Theory X concept is based on the view that the employees are lazy and would avoid work if possible; therefore, close supervision is imperative. Hence, theory X managers are viewed as authoritarian.

The theory Y concept identifies workers as ambitious and highly self-motivated. Hence theory Y managers need to facilitate the work environment to such a standard that enables workers to thrive and supersede their ambition and drive.

Theory Z was proposed by Ouchi; his theory was that offering job security was the way for businesses to forge ahead. The results of this lead to high performance and job satisfaction.

FW Taylor's theory of motivation is viewed as the father of scientific management theory. His time and motion study focused on critically analysing every minute bit of the employee tasks.

FW Taylor proposed that the ability of the business to have qualified and adequately trained employees who could create new ideas was the key to the progress of the business. Such employees could then perform at their maximum efficiency. Furthermore, he suggested that managers should be able to apply scientific principles to planning of work and tasks for the subordinates.

Abraham Maslow's theory of motivation is known as the hierarchy of needs. This identifies these needs as physiological need, safety, social or belonging needs, esteem or self-respect and self-actualisation.

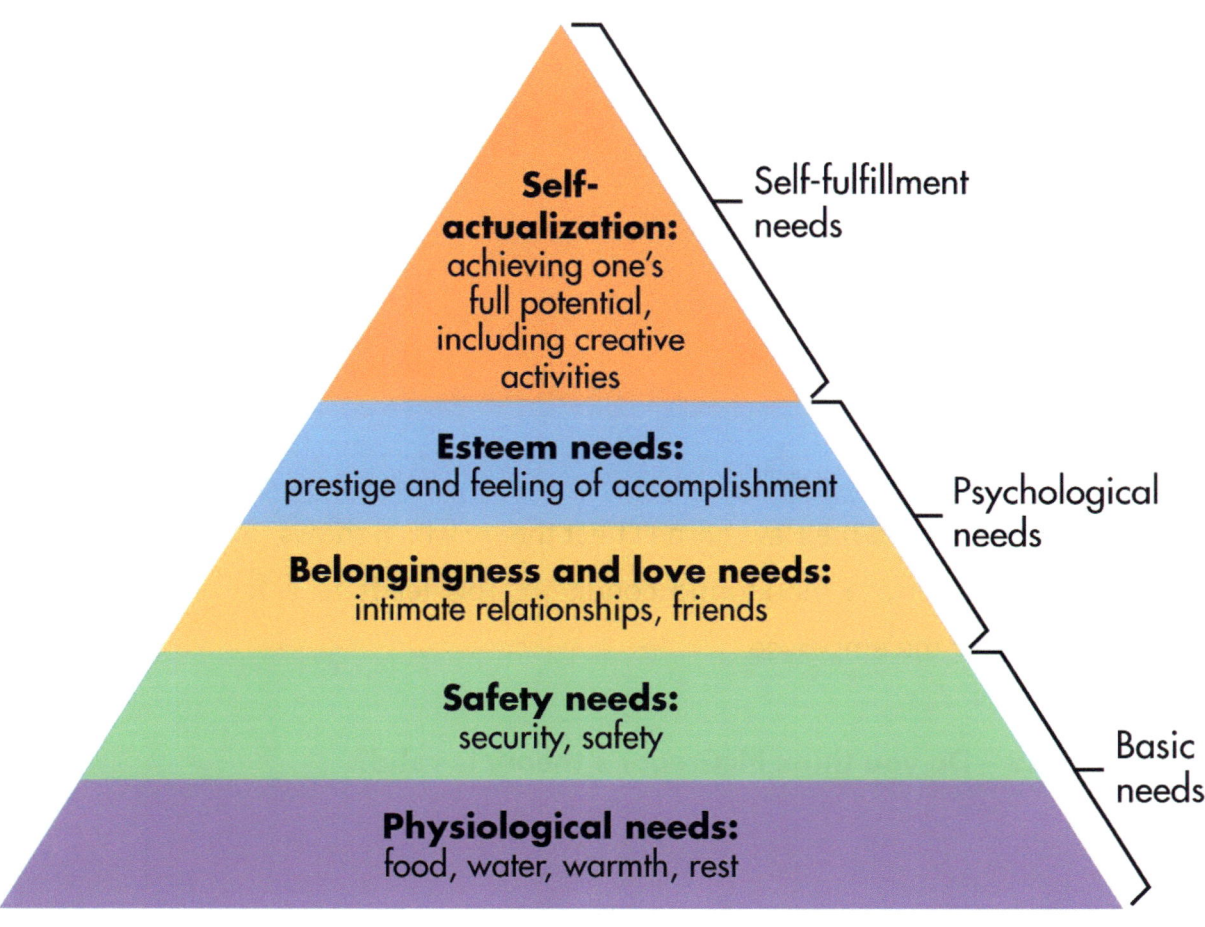

Frederick Herzberg identified the two-factor theory which was based on satisfaction and dissatisfaction. Motivators increased satisfaction, and de-motivators reduced job satisfaction. Motivators include growth, recognition, responsibility, achievement, the actual work and promotion.

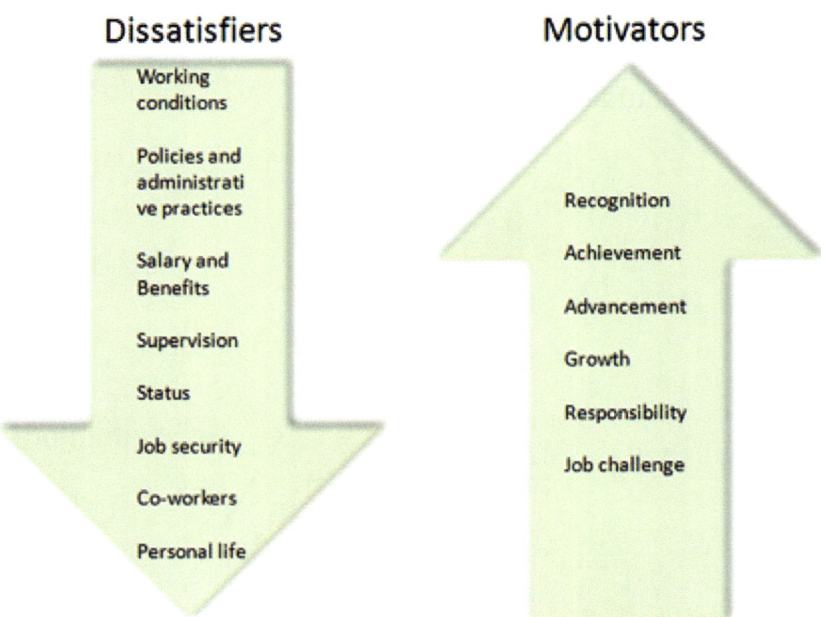

Elton Mayo proposed the Hawthorne Effect theory which shows temporary motivation of people under close monitoring condition. This leads to a temporary change in performance of the employee.

**Activity 19 – Do you think McGregor's theory is valid?**

## Organisational Structure and Motivational Techniques

There are four main forms of organisational structure and motivational techniques which include:

- Entrepreneurial
- Bureaucratic
- Matrix
- Independence

In 1985, an academic named Charles Handy (drawing on the earlier work of Roger Harrison in 1974) developed a four-fold classification model of how companies organise themselves. Handy's four-fold model is roughly as follows:

### Entrepreneurial structure

The emphasis of this structure is central power. This form of organisational structure is like a spider's web, or the spokes of a bicycle wheel with the project manager, CEO, MD or other person in overall charge right in the centre, and everyone radiating out from him, and therefore everyone reporting to him. It is a very flat structure with very few layers. This form of structure will only have a chance of succeeding if the organisation or project is relatively small.

New or young organisations often have this format, and develop into something different as they grow in size and complexity. A huge and complex organisation will always be beyond the scope of a single individual, however talented, to maintain control of everyone and have everyone report directly to him.

Within this structure there are few collective decisions taken during meetings and a greater degree of autonomy is given to individuals. Flair and rapid decision makers thrive in this sort of environment, even if they are not at the very centre of the structure.

Accounts

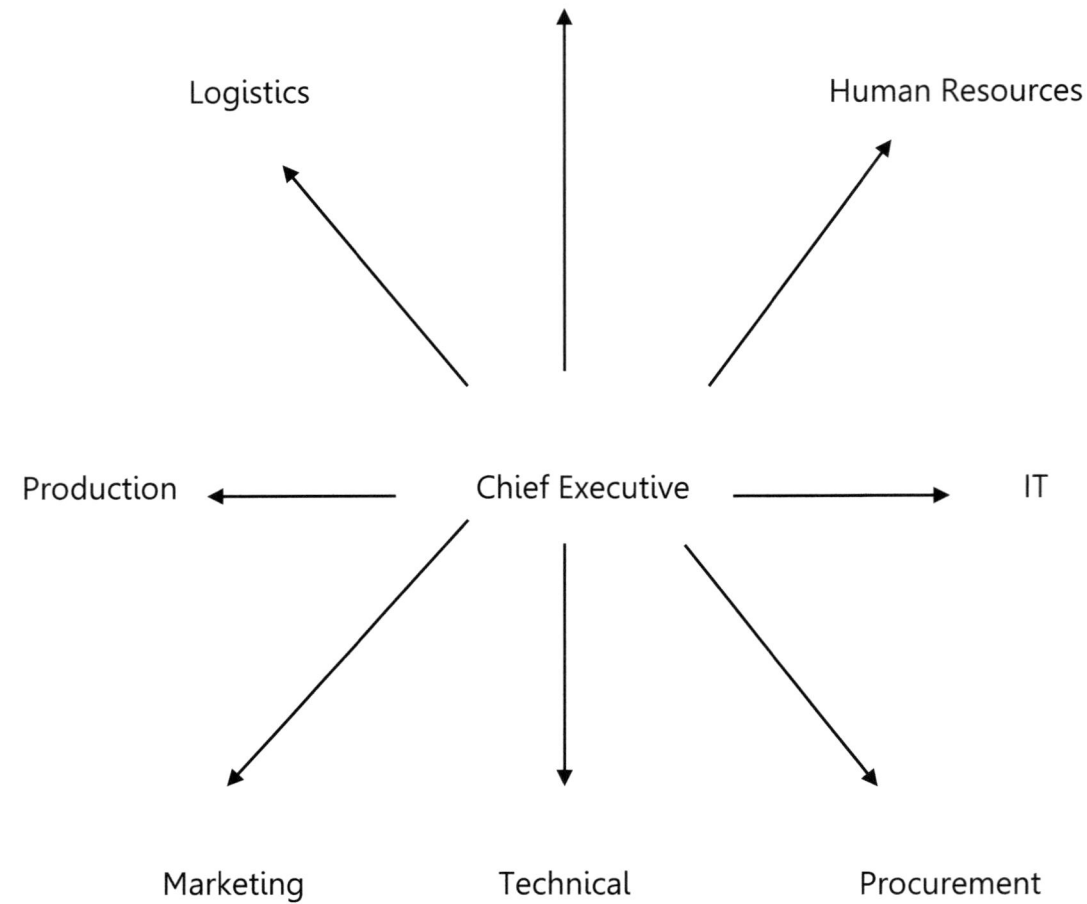

**Activity 20 – Do you think the entrepreneurial structure is practical?**

**Bureaucratic structure**

The bureaucratic form of organisational structure is intended to highlight precisely where power is distributed within an organisation. It easily highlights who is responsible for a section, who he reports to and who reports to him. This form of structure is frequently used and often called a "family tree" for obvious reasons. Larger organisations that have grown beyond the entrepreneurial form tend to move towards the bureaucratic structure as it is perceived to offer more control of the company. It is very much a top down structure where the person sitting at the top is obviously the person in charge. This type of structure emphasises the role, rather than individual flair, and there is less scope for individuals to demonstrate initiative outside of their defined role. This form tends to produce more stability in an organisation, although less flexibility. Committees tend to replace individual freedom. This form of structure has tended to be the norm throughout human history – we tend to be a hierarchical species and prefer to know who is in charge and where we sit in the chain of command, although it certainly does not suit everyone or every organisation.

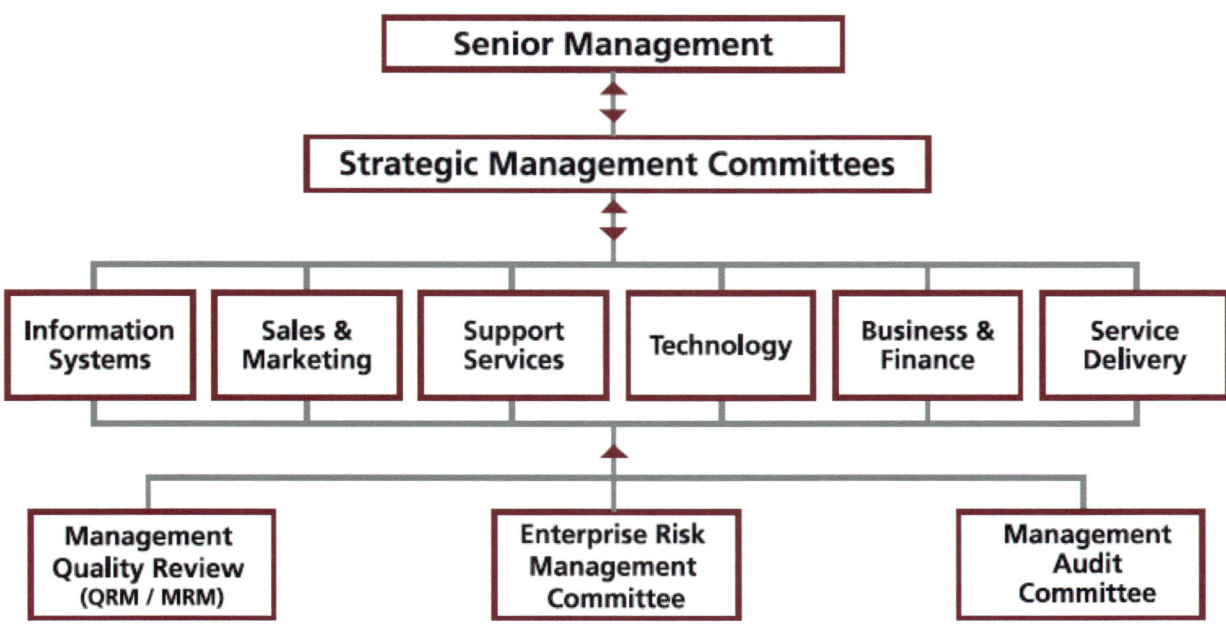

## Matrix

The matrix form of organisational structure tries to emphasise the coordination and cooperation of the various skills, knowledge and expertise of everyone within the organisation, or within the project team. It was developed in an attempt to try and overcome some of the difficulties of the bureaucratic and entrepreneurial structures. This structure makes inter-departmental cooperation more apparent, and is especially useful for projects where you do not always want a rigid managerial structure, but want individuals with the ability and willingness to maintain some of the flexibility of the entrepreneurial form whilst still achieving some of the discipline of the bureaucratic organisation. This form of structure tends to appeal to most thinking managers on a theoretical level as it allows people at a very junior level (perhaps graduates for example) to have an input at a much higher level if they have some particular skill that is required. Organisations, particularly large ones, tend to shy away from this form because it tends to be more expensive as more support staff are usually required, e.g. secretaries etc. to keep track of what becomes an unwieldy administrative system.

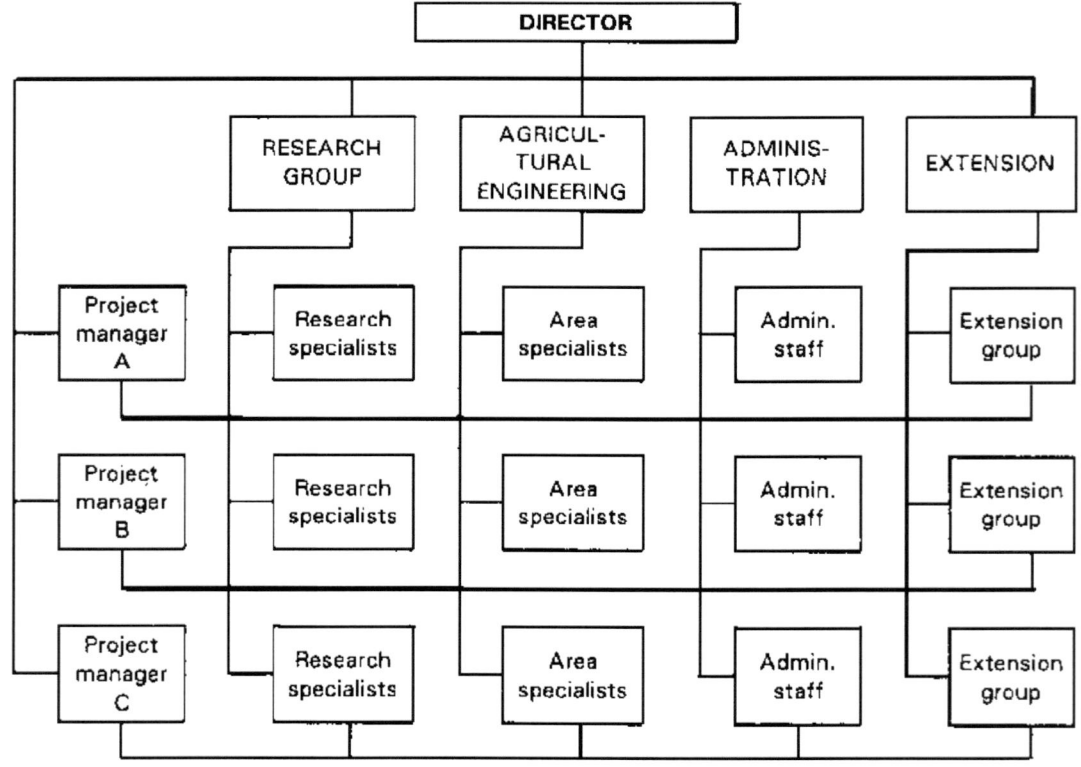

**Independence form**

The independence form of organisational structure emphasises the individual even more so than the entrepreneurial form and in some ways seems to be anti the very concept of organisation.

The first three forms of structure all attempt to bring together the skills and knowledge of individuals to try and produce synergism and a situation in which the whole is greater than the sum of the parts. In the independence form the idea is to produce a system which allows individuals to perform to their full potential with only minimal support.

The individuals are usually experts in their field and tend not to require input from others to perform their jobs. Doctors' surgeries and barristers' chambers often operate in this way as it is particularly suited to independently minded experts who are confident in their own ability.

**Activity 21 – Think of an organisation you are familiar with. Which organisation type is it, and does it work?**

**Leadership**

A leader is someone who has a vision for the future direction of the business, someone who inspires other to follow, shows the ability to make decisions and commands respect. Whereas a manager is responsible for the day to day running of the business, delegating roles and responsibilities and ensuring the smooth running.

There are a number of leadership styles:

- Autocratic – this is where the leaders have all the power and decision making; there is little employee consultation and communication is top down
- Paternalistic – is where the leader decides what is best for the employees almost taking on the role of a parent; there is little delegation and the leader is likely to explain to the employees why the decision has been taken
- Democratic – this is where leadership and decisions are taken as a group; employees have greater involvement and the emphasis is on delegation and consultation. Employees feel valued and this leads to greater levels of motivation
- Laissez-faire – this is where the managers and employees have freedom to do what they think is best; the leader has little input into the day to day decision making and there is poor role definition for managers

**Self-assessment questions:**

1) Explain the methods of development and retention of an effective workforce.
2) Discuss the financial methods of motivation used by businesses.
3) Highlight the components of an effective job design.
4) Outline the various theories of motivation. What is the relevance of each respective theory in business?

**Topic 1.5 - Entrepreneurs and Leaders**

**Learning Outcome**

The aim of this section is for students to understand the following:

- Role of an Entrepreneur
- Entrepreneurial Motives and Characteristics
- Business Objectives
- Forms of Business
- Business Choices
- Moving from Entrepreneur to Leader

**Role of an Entrepreneur**

The aims of this unit are to enable you to:

- Know about starting a business enterprise
- Risks and rewards of setting out to be an entrepreneur
- Support available from the government

**Starting a Business**

**Introduction**

This is the introductory unit to this A-level, and in it you will learn the main concepts of business, and what it involves.

In business it is vital to have new and innovative ideas, to be creative and to have the right skill-set.

Entrepreneurs can take many different forms; it can be an individual taking on fresh and new challenges; it could be a new venture for a large company (driven by individuals) or it could simply be an individual with inspiration. It is almost always driven by an individual, however.

Entrepreneurship is very vital to UK economy. Since the end of the Second World War in 1945, new and small businesses have been responsible for providing approximately 95% of the radical innovations in the economy.

There are potential risks involved with starting a business, but there are also huge potential rewards. Entrepreneurs can create a great deal of wealth for themselves, their business and employees and the government as the business grows favourably. There is no guarantee of success, however.

There are costs associated with every business decision. A sensible business will establish this cost before making a business decision, particularly when the cost is likely to be significant, as with a major new investment or expansion.

However large the company or wealthy the individual, there will always be a limited amount of available capital to invest in a new venture. The entrepreneur must decide, based on sound financial planning, where to best invest their money and time; there will always be many calls upon both.

Even given the potential problems and liabilities, there is never a shortage of potential entrepreneurs willing to take risks for the potential rewards that they hope awaits them.

There are tremendous benefits of becoming an entrepreneur. These include attaining financial independence, freedom to make own decisions and realising one's dreams, goals and strengths, among many others.

Provided the right steps and the right courses of actions are taken by the enterprise/entrepreneur, the sky's the limit to what can be achieved.

**Activity 22 – In your own words describe what an entrepreneur is.**

**What is a Business Enterprise?**

A business enterprise usually takes on different meanings depending on who is using it, and in what context.

It could be an organisation specifically established for business activities: limited companies are an example of this.

It can be viewed from the perspective of the ability of a discerning individual to embark upon new challenges, be inspirational, original and innovative. The ability to combine all the above traits to successfully run a business effectively is what makes an enterprise.

**Entrepreneurial Motives and Characteristics**

**The Business Entrepreneur**

If an enterprise is to be a success, the entrepreneur needs to be able to make excellent decisions and to be able to apply them to solve problems. Just having good ideas is not enough: you need to be able to implement them.

The term entrepreneur has various facets and is not limited to starting a business. It could also involve reinventing an already existing business and turning it into a much more competitive and highly profitable enterprise; for example, Sir Stelios Haji-Ioannou, the founder of EasyJet.

Another category of entrepreneurs start single or multiple businesses based on similar brand names, strategies and techniques which they utilise in the expansion of their businesses. A typical example in this case would be the Virgin group of Companies founded by Sir Richard Branson. Today, the Virgin group is involved in telecommunications, banking, cable television, air travel and rail travel amongst others.

It is very characteristic of entrepreneurs to take high risks in starting up businesses. Such risks could stem from their outright belief in the potential for profitability of a product which they perceive to be a potential success story. In cases like these, such entrepreneurs go against the odds to establish their enterprise.

Of course, with high risks are possibly high levels of return. However, the nature of the risks are what set entrepreneurs apart. The risks and rewards in entrepreneurship are covered in greater depth in the next section.

There are fourteen key characteristics of successful business entrepreneurs which are essential for making the enterprise viable and profitable:

- Self-confidence
- Low fear of failure
- Drive and Energy
- High Initiative and Personal Responsibility
- Moderate risk-taking
- Good use of feedback
- Self-imposed standards
- Clear goal setting
- Good use of resources
- Money seen as a measure, not merely as an end
- Continuous problem solving
- Tolerance of ambiguity
- Long-term involvement
- Internal locus of control

These traits were identified by Jeffrey Timmons of the Massachusetts Institute of Technology.

You should note that this is an ideal list, and not everyone will possess every trait. Some will succeed in some areas more than others. Other research studies have highlighted the need for a sense of achievement, self-confidence and persistence as very crucial in becoming a successful entrepreneur.

Leadership is clearly a character trait that should underpin every decision-making capability in order to drive any enterprise to success.

This has been reinforced by several authors at various intervals:

- In 1959, by A Cole
- In 1961 by D McClelland
- In 1970 by J Collins
- In 1990s by B Bird

Entrepreneurs are economically very important. Developed economies have high levels of competitiveness and innovation which are brought about by a high level of entrepreneurial activity. It is not a surprise to note that economies with buoyant levels of such entrepreneurial activity thrive and are more productive in terms of levels of growth and wealth creation.

For example, an estimated 4.5 million businesses were established by the end of 2010 as a direct result of entrepreneurial activities. The effect of this would mean:

- The creation of jobs
- The enhancement of modern technology and its use in new product development and services
- Increase in export earnings
- Greater production of goods and services
- Higher tax revenue for central government

**Risks and Rewards**

**Potential Risks**

All businesses carry potential risks and rewards. It is the responsibility of the entrepreneur to gauge the levels of risks to be taken against the prospective returns to ascertain whether or not a given risk is worth taking and if the potential reward is worth the associated risk.

In broad terms, the greater the risks, the greater the potential rewards. This is, of course, a little simplistic and is not always the case. It is therefore important that a good entrepreneur can identify business opportunities and take reasonable levels of risks without jeopardising the business enterprise.

There are some important questions an entrepreneur needs to ask before deciding to take certain risks:

- What is my general attitude to risk?
- Can the business deal with the risk?
- Are there better alternatives to taking the risk which have not yet been explored?
- Does the situation absolutely warrant taking the risk?
- What is the cost and affordability of this risk for the business?

The process of risk management is an absolute necessity which must not be overlooked, however large your business. It critically examines the risks which could incur or exacerbate tremendous losses to the business, and the greatest possible likelihood of such losses occurring.

The entrepreneur endeavours to mitigate such risks and potential losses by following some simple steps:

- Identifying the risks
- Quantifying the risk
- Managing and mitigating the risk

After these have been identified, there are four different actions which can be taken to manage risks:

- The first action is to reduce the risk; this can involve both reducing the likelihood of a loss occurring AND reducing the size of a loss if it does occur. This can help to safeguard the business as a whole from losses that are inevitable
- The transfer of risk involves using a third party in order to remove the risk directly from the business. A typical example of this is through the use of insurance to reduce risk or offset any loss
- Avoidance of risks which simply advocates that any risky venture should be completely avoided. For example, not setting up your business in an area with a high burglary crime rate because there are very high chances that the business would be targeted on several occasions
- Risk Retention designates that some risks are bound to happen and some point and there is nothing that could have been done to prevent it. An example is when a major supplier goes into administration and becomes bankrupt; plans can be in place, however, to mitigate this, such as having alternative suppliers ready

**Potential rewards**

As a start-up business, the entrepreneur may have limited resources at their disposal; however, with this risk potential comes the possible reward of developing an extensive network of clients, partners, suppliers and other networks. The benefits of this reward opportunity can only be explored by taking the risk of networking, having realised the resource limitations which already exist and seeing networking as the opportunity to counteract such limitations.

The vast amount of work responsibilities and tasks which have to be done due to the very nature of small businesses provides the chance for a knowledge of a wide range of work challenges. Although there may not be a set or defined job description, which is a potential risk that the entrepreneur is willing to take, the reward of such risks is the outcome of success and the pride, joy and sense of accomplishment which comes with achieving success.

**Activity 23 – What sort of risks do you think entrepreneurs take?**

**Business Choices**

An entrepreneur will look for a gap in the market which they can exploit to their advantage and be successful. The choice of business will depend on the entrepreneur's previous experiences, their areas of expertise or skills base and also the opportunities made available to them. They will evaluate the options and then this will determine the business choice they make.

**Opportunity Cost**

Definition

Opportunity cost is what the business enterprise has to forego and give up in order to actually accomplish the business decision and path that has been chosen. It is the 'opportunity' that could have been taken but had to be forfeited in order to apply the choice of the business plan you have chosen.

There are numerous alternatives which the entrepreneur must choose from. From these options the best choice must be made in order to optimise resources, maximise profits and minimise risks.

New business start-ups encounter another form of opportunity cost: the cost of borrowing the initial funds in order to commence business operations.

The interest payment which they would have to pay towards the cost of borrowing these funds on a monthly basis are in actual fact an opportunity cost – money that could be used elsewhere, and therefore a foregone alternative.

This monthly outgoing can be viewed as a loss to the business. It could have been used to invest in other resources for the business, had the enterprise not borrowed the money of which they now have to repay with the interest.

## Implications of opportunity costs

The concept of opportunity cost has a number of implications which affect businesses. For every lost opportunity, in order for that opportunity to have been profitable, the business would have to have chosen the best investment decision to yield profitability and high returns. Always remember that resources are scarce, and hence there is a limited supply which makes the scope of choice imperative.

Even for a very wealthy entrepreneur, choices still need to be made, and every business decision taken means that possibilities are rejected and opportunities lost. This cost is not the sum of all the foregone alternatives. Instead it is a measure of the benefit which could have been received from the next best.

Even governments have limited resources and have to deal with the far-reaching consequences of the choices that they make. Therefore they have to give up projects which in their very nature would be beneficial in several ways to the economy, in order to meet the demands of projects which have been given a higher priority.

In a business context, there may be limited production capacity, limitations on the human resource, on technology etc. The list is potentially very long of limiting factors. For example, if an enterprise is considering the production of a new synthetic beauty product, more of the existing resources would be diverted from the beauty product range, leading to potential difficulties there. The opportunity cost of the beauty product would then be the other products which have not been produced.

We can see that the opportunity cost concept is applicable on all levels: national, all levels of business and on a personal level. For every choice there is usually a good alternative that would have to be forfeited (this ties in with risk management, of course). Ideally, whichever option is selected must be the best choice for the business.

**Becoming an Entrepreneur**

Sometimes individuals are motivated to become entrepreneurs in order to gain a greater degree of independence and freedom – both financial and personal.

Humans are creative animals, and are adept at spotting opportunities in markets and developing ideas and products to satisfy those opportunities.

As part of the re-evaluation of individual progress, it is also a common desire to contribute to attempt to make a positive impact on society as a whole. This attitude tends to create entrepreneurs who are willing to offer some of the benefits they gain to society at large, or to specific areas in the society that they may feel an affinity with.

**Spotting a gap in the market**

The entrepreneur is always searching for a gap in the market which they can exploit with a new product or service. It does not have to be an area of specialisation for the entrepreneur.

In our information age, and with the vast amount of information readily available, it is not hard to spot the market gaps, although ones that can become large businesses are more difficult.

The difference between the entrepreneur and the average individual is that the average individual is usually not particularly diligent in searching out these opportunities, and hence misses out on the very rare opportunities which the discerning entrepreneur would be quick to grab. Even when they are spotted the average person doesn't have the vision to exploit them.

It is worthy of note that a major opportunity has to fill a real gap in the market. These market gaps are created by any of the following reasons:

- The lack of quality products available
- Consumers need a new product or service
- Limited supply in the market for a given product or service
- Cheaper products required (or on occasion more expensive luxury items)

So, if your new idea can fill the gap in the existing market, the next thing to do is confirm that this is a genuine opportunity. For example, every Christmas a particular children's toy captures the imagination of a generation of children and sells extremely well. This does not mean a new range of similar toys would do well; it could just be a limited time fad.

Some questions to consider would be:

- How long is this opportunity expected to last in the long-term or short-term?
- Which market is available for this opportunity?
- Is it definitely possible to make a product or service which will adequately fill the market gap?
- What information is available on this opportunity, and is it sufficient or is more needed?
- What proof is there to show that this is a truly genuine opportunity and not a hoax?
- What are the risks involved?
- Are the potential rewards greater than the potential risks?

**Development of innovative and new products and processes**

The discerning entrepreneurial mind can spot distinct market gaps and looks for the best ideas and processes to make these ideas become reality, and to fill those gaps.

With more than 80% failures of new market ideas in practice, it cannot be over-emphasised how important it is to know about the markets for which these new ideas are designed.

You must also very clearly understand your intended market, be they other businesses, the government or consumers. Your venture is likely to fail if you do not know your market thoroughly.

You also need to be fully aware of the competition in the market place you are entering. All these factors can clearly be known by the entrepreneur through a carefully conducted campaign of market research.

**Activity 24 – Think of a market. Can you think of any gaps in that market that a new product or service might exploit?**

**Activity 25 - Log onto the internet and read this article about a well-known Dragon's Den entrepreneur:**
http://businesscasestudies.co.uk/bannatyne/from-ice-cream-van-to-dragons-den-duncan-bannatyne/introduction

http://www.bbc.co.uk/dragonsden/entrepreneurs/

**Business Objectives**

Small businesses such as those set up by entrepreneurs have several objectives, these include:

- Survival – a significant amount of new businesses will fail within the first year of creation.
- Profit maximisation – the start-up costs for a new business are high and so a new business will want a high return on its investment.
- Sales maximisation and market share – sell as many products or services as possible and secure a share of the market to gain competitive advantage
- Cost efficiency – small businesses such as those set up by entrepreneurs generally cannot benefit from economies of scale, however, they will want to keep costs as low as possible
- Employee welfare – small businesses who employee staff will work closely with those staff who will be a big part of helping the business grow. Their welfare is important as they will be considered as one of the family for their role in this.
- Customer satisfaction – by keeping the customers happy the business can depend on repeat sales and also increase their market share
- Social objectives – the outcomes for individuals and the community of the business

Business enterprises are always a positive way forward for the economy in several ways:

- New business start-ups provide new products and services to the economy
- They alleviate the unemployment problem and create new jobs
- They reduce the welfare budget by reducing unemployment
- These businesses generate revenue for the government through the payment of tax
- They improve our exports
- They help attract the best minds from around the world to work in the UK

Enterprises benefit the economy in terms of increased employment and the tax paid to the exchequer. Governments are always very keen to offer support and advice to entrepreneurs in order to help them achieve their business objectives.

There are several organisations which have been set up to ensure that the needs of various businesses are met. These organisations are regulated and provide information, funding and support, and advise businesses on different issues in order to improve their competitiveness.

In 2007, the Department for Business, Enterprise and Regulatory Reform (DBERR) was established. It was responsible for the creation of conditions for businesses to succeed. It has now been superseded by the Department for Business Innovation & Skills:

https://www.gov.uk/government/organisations/department-for-business-innovation-skills

The Department for Business, Innovation & Skills (BIS) is the department for economic growth. The department invests in skills and education to promote trade, boost innovation and help people to start and grow a business. BIS also protects consumers and reduces the impact of regulation.

BIS is a ministerial department, supported by 45 agencies and public bodies.

The Department of Innovation, Universities and Skills (DIUS) was another major initiative specifically designed to promote business research, propelling enterprise and efficiency, and the creation of new products and services. Many academics, however, saw the hiving off of universities from the education department as a retrograde step. This department was subsequently absorbed into the BIS.

Regional Development Agencies (RDAs) were established with statutory objectives which they were required to provide by law. Their requirements were:

- The enhancement of business competitiveness and efficiency
- Promote employment
- Contribute to sustainable economic development
- Foster the development and application of skills which are relevant to employment
- Promote economic development and regeneration

However, they too were abolished with effect from March 2012, with no replacement planned.

N.B. With all such initiatives and bodies set up with a mission in mind, it is essential for students to be aware of their probable demise or reforming. As we can see above, different governments will see things differently from their predecessors and will wish to make their own mark, even if the method of doing so remains fundamentally the same. So please do your research to ensure you have up-to-date information in this regard.

**Government departments and agencies**

Part of the responsibility of the government to ensure that enterprises are well-regulated and informed as to the best business actions that would derive the greatest benefits to both the business and the economy at large. For example, it is in no one's interests to create products or services which increase pollution or can endanger lives and the environment in any form.

Hence, in order to achieve the optimum benefits of businesses, the government provides:

- Specific business support for enterprises involved in the exportation of products and services
- Training programmes which provide enlightenment and information on a wide variety of business issues
- Grants aimed at promoting development, especially in deprived regions with high unemployment rates

As mentioned above, this is a constantly changing environment, and what was available today may not be when you read this.

**Activity 26 – Why do you think governments seek to support entrepreneurs?**

**How to get Support**

All businesses, and especially new ones, need to operate in the most effective and efficient way possible to reduce costs and the avoidable risks.

A good first step for an entrepreneur is to have an action plan, more commonly called a business plan.

This document will outline the purpose and intentions of the business and the future goals which it aims to achieve. Such plans give the enterprise clarity of purpose and a solid set of goals and objectives. They can easily identify the target market, products and services to be offered, the information on the competition plus information on funding.

The following organisations can provide good advice to entrepreneurs:

- The Chamber of Commerce
- High-street banks

They can provide support, advice, grants, and development funds in particular parts of the country. For instance, where funding is concerned, banks can provide business overdraft facilities and low interest-rate loan facilities.

**Moving from an Entrepreneur to a Leader**

Eventually the business will grow into a size where more than one person (the entrepreneur) can no longer effectively manage the business. The entrepreneur needs to detach themselves from the emotional side of the organisation to become a manager. This will mean learning how to delegate and trust and verify staff who may have assisted in the business start-up but who now do not have the skills required to grow the business. The entrepreneur will need to learn to be less spontaneous with a gut-reaction approach to business and develop financial and strategic plans. It can be difficult for an entrepreneur to become a leader as it requires that they let go of some of the day to day running of the business and entrust their business to someone else, who does not necessarily have the same investment in the business. However, it is vital that the entrepreneur does that in order for the businesses survival and success.

**Self-assessment questions:**

1) Identify the potential risks and rewards in establishing a business enterprise.
2) Explain how you might spot a gap in the market.
3) How might you seek help and advice, and from what sources?

**Forms of business**

There are many forms of business, the type that a business employs depends on the number of people involved, the financial investment and the nature of the business.

Most small business will start off as a sole trader, where the owner invests their own personal funds. It is easy to set up and does not require lengthy legal paperwork. However, the owner is responsible for all of the businesses debts.

Professional businesses such as accountants and lawyers with several individuals setting up the business together will create a partnership. This is a legally binding form with a Deed of partnership that sets out each partner's investment and role or responsibility. Partnerships can have limited liability, where each partner is only responsible for their own investment.

A larger or growing business will have greater expenses and individuals will want to protect their personal assets. By becoming a limited liability business they can do this.

Individuals may want the freedom that owning their own business provides, but want to minimise the risk of setting up a new business. This can be achieved through purchasing a franchise, where individuals buy into an existing and successful business such as Subway for an initial investment and a share of the profits. In return they get to trade under a well-established name with the benefits of support.

Social enterprises are businesses or activities set up to benefit the local community in which they operate. They are generally not set up with profit maximisation as the main objective. Lifestyle business are very fashionable and are clearly linked in with trends and fashions such the current craze of the benefits of Aloe Vera to health.

The largest of the forms of business is a Public limited company (PLC). This type of ownership offers limited liability and is floated on the stock market, where anyone can purchase shares in the business.

# Theme 2

# Managing Business Activities

Topic 2.1 - Raising Finance

Topic 2.2 - Financial Planning

Topic 2.3 - Managing Finance

Topic 2.4 - Resource Management

Topic 2.5 - External Influences

**Topic 2.1 - Raising Finance**

**Learning Outcome**

The aim of this section is for students to understand the following:

- Internal Finance
- External Finance
- Liability
- Planning

## Internal and External Finance

Even after the initial business capital is secured, a business needs to continually have the finance to carry out its day-to-day activities.

Businesses can acquire finance through internal or external sources. Internal sources are from inside the business and can include retained profits, sale of assets such as premises or machinery and the business owners' funds/savings. External sources are from outside of the business and can include bank loans and sources of capital.

The type of business, the state of the economy and the stage of the development of the business affect the sources of finance that are available to the business.

With established companies, it is easier to secure funding from multiple sources at a low risk for the financiers and lenders. However, smaller businesses are seen as a greater risk and can find it more difficult to obtain credit.

Smaller businesses may look to obtain finance through friends and family who will lend money with preferable conditions for repayment such as low or nil interest rates and also a flexible repayment plan.

Peer to peer funding allows individuals to choose who they would like to lend money to and assign an appropriate rate of interest dependent on the perceived risk to the individual of lending to the business.

Business angels are individuals with disposable income who wish to support a business with their start-up costs for a share in the business.

Crowd funding is asking a large group of people to invest a small amount of money into a business.

**Activity 27 – Do some quick research on venture capital. What is it?**

**Venture Capital**

This is a source of finance that is provided to the business that guarantees long-term share capital.

Venture capital is provided by private investors both to start-up and expanding businesses.

In exchange for the capital, a private investor receives a share of the business. In addition, the investor receives a return on the investment (ROI) that depends on profit from the growth of the business.

Venture capitalists tend to have a major influence in any business in which they invest. They can be very demanding in terms of the control they wish to exert.

The business owner needs to weigh this potential interference when bringing venture capitalists on board. It also needs to be considered, of course, that the venture capitalists might bring expertise that the business does not possess.

Another factor which the owner should consider is the percentage of profit demanded by the venture capitalist. The greater the venture capital invested, the higher the expectations on return on investment. They can ultimately control the company.

**Bank Loans and Overdrafts**

A bank loan can be taken out by a business to finance its activities. The business can borrow a specified sum of money from a bank with regular and set repayments for a specified period of time.

The bank charges an interest on this loan and will often require collateral to secure the loan, in the event of failure to repay the loan. Longer term loans have higher interests on them. Bank overdrafts are another option, but these tend to be smaller in scale and designed to get over short-term cash flow issues.

The overdraft is a set limit and that is the maximum the business can withdraw from its bank account for its business activities. It is vital that any business that takes out a loan or an overdraft meets its repayments.

The business needs to decide carefully which is appropriate, loans or overdrafts, as they will each carry different conditions. Overdrafts, for example, tend to carry much higher interest rate repayments.

Business owners need to think carefully about cash flow issues, and how to manage them (e.g. loans, overdrafts etc.). Many perfectly good businesses fail because they do not manage their cash flow effectively.

Businesses can limit their need for finance through leasing equipment or premises rather than purchasing them out right.

Having an arrangement with suppliers in the form of trade credit can allow a business to have goods and services and pay for them at a later date, generally 30, 60 or 90 days after receiving them. Depending on the type of business, and its location the business may be eligible for grants to help them start–up as they will provide products and services and jobs to the local area. These grants do not have to be repaid.

**Personal Sources**

Owners of small businesses often invest their own money into their business. This money could come from:

- Personal savings
- Inherited funds
- Selling of personal assets
- Taking out personal bank loans

They do this because they want the business to survive and grow. It is quite challenging for a small business to get credit for financing it; hence the reliance on personal funds.

The ultimate risk is that any business can fail, and the owner loses their personal assets.

**Activity 28 – What is the major risk of an individual investing their own money rather than acquiring finances from another source?**

**Liability**

**Ordinary Share Capital**

Limited Companies issue shares to investors as a means of raising capital. In return, the investors receive a portion of the company, which is equivalent to the amount of shares purchased. The business uses the flotation of shares to make its shares available to the general public for sale.

There are two types of shares:

- Ordinary Shares
- Preference Shares

Ordinary shares are sold to the investor who in return receives a portion of the profits that the company makes. This is given in the form of a dividend which changes annually to reflect the performance of the business.

Preference shares are given to preferential investors at a fixed dividend rate, regardless of the performance of the business. These preferential shareholders are always paid before the ordinary shareholders.

Issuing ordinary shares tends to reduce the power of ownership of the original owners of the business as it reduces their relative shareholding. Unless the business owners retain 51% of the business, they could risk losing control of the whole business to its shareholders.

An unlimited company is where the owners are responsible for all debt such as a sole trader, if the company fails then the owner may have to sell their personal possessions such as their house in order to repay the debt. Whereas, in a limited company the owners are not responsible for the debt. A limited company has its own legal identity, and this means the owners are not personally responsible for the organisation's debt.

The liability of the business will determine the type of finance that they can access, dependent on the risk factors.

**Self-assessment questions:**

1) How do businesses raise finance?
2) What are the different sources of finance for the business?
3) Highlight the benefits and drawbacks of the various sources of finance.

**Business Planning**

**Introduction**

In this section we will look at the basis for setting the objectives and goals of a business into visible action. Documenting goals and systems gives the entrepreneur (and the business) a clear focus on the future direction of the business. Whenever there seems to be a deviation from the stated objectives of the business, an action plan makes it easier to understand where the business is failing by identifying the weaknesses and then implementing a swift process to recover and set the business right back on track.

The business plan defines the business and gives the prospective reader an impression of the organisation. The first impression may be the only impression created of the business; therefore, the business needs to make sure it is a true representation of what it stands for.

Investors, creditors and lenders, prospective business partners are among the potential readers of the business plan. Therefore, it is imperative that any business plan is robust, accurate, well written and can survive thorough scrutiny.

A vast wealth of information and support is available to entrepreneurs looking to establish businesses. Government organisations, trade associations, confederations and many more are sources of information and support for businesses. These organisations have advisory services available, websites and a host of other links which are designed to provide excellent services to businesses.

Business planning involves a lot of hard work and organisation. This unit identifies the merits of planning and how it is beneficial to the business. The shortcomings and pitfalls to avoid are also covered.

A business plan is a document which details the following:

- The businesses objectives
- Plans
- Strategies
- Financial forecasts
- The market in which the business would be operating

Its primary aim is to provide an overview of the company in order to secure financial backing and funding from financial institutions and prospective investors. A business plan is also used as an instrument of measurement to compare the actual performance of the business to forecasted figures.

Business plans provide essential information on how the business is expected to take-off and develop. It is also important to give achievable timescales for the goals that are set. Unachievable timescales will make you look unprofessional.

Since it is important for the business to acquire funds and financial support, the business plan must show how money invested intends to be properly managed, and that there are adequate accountability measures in place.

This gives the business a high level of credibility because any potential investor knows that in the near future, it will be reaping the rewards of investing in the business.

The executive summary introduces the business plan and contains the vital information needed to gain the attention of any investor. It should be precise and a maximum of two pages.

The other key elements of the business plan should include:

- Description of the proposed business
- Business marketing and sales strategy
- Operations information including location, production and infrastructure
- Forecasts figures

The proposed business must be clearly explained in the business plan, including the activities of the business, and its goals for the near future. It includes also the following:

- The business start date
- Sector in which it would be categorised
- History of the business
- Legal structure

The product details and services offered need to be very clear on the following information:

- Unique attributes of the product
- Target market
- Relevant information on the sector
- Patents, trademarks, design rights as applicable

The features of the market place must be very clear:

- Market niche and basis for identifying such a market
- Competition in the market place and who the major players are
- Characteristics of the market including current issues affecting the market, development and size of the market

Marketing methods, sales tactics and financial forecasts are crucial information which must be practical and achievable:

- How will potential customers be identified and targeted?
- The methods of positioning the business to have a favourable competitive advantage
- Pricing policy – standard for all customers or flexible to adapt to different customers
- Distribution process for the products to reach consumers
- Sales tactics to be utilised – face-to-face, website, telephone or otherwise

Details of the financial figures and amount for starting-up the business need to be precise, accurate and very clear:

- Forecast on profit and loss which estimates the sales projections, the costs involved in production and expenses and business running costs or overheads
- Cash-flow statement – with flow of cash in and out of the business for the first twelve months
- Sales forecast – anticipated income from the sale of products

**Activity 29 – Outline what you would put in a business plan.**

## Cash-Flow Forecasting

In any business enterprise, one of the most tangible asset it has is cash, although the actual value of that cash does change, especially in relation to other currencies.

Given the importance of cash, it is important to forecast the flow of cash into and out of the business. The cash-flow is used to monitor the business activities.

Cash in any business is used to meet daily expenses, bills and lots more besides. Failure to have a steady flow of cash could result in setbacks and unnecessary delays to the effective functioning of the business. The dire consequences of failure of steady stream cash-flow can result in business failure.

## Importance of cash-flow forecasts

- Providing advance cash for a business
- Manipulating expenditure and income accounts to cover the likelihood of failures and shortfalls
- Forecasting provides insight into possible avenues which need to be tightened to prevent cash-flow problems

## Forecasting Cash Flow

There are two columns of any cash-flow forecast:

- The first one lists the actual amount of the cash-flow forecast
- The second column lists the forecast amount

A standard forecast lists the following information:

- Balance between receipts and payments with the negative figures shown in brackets
- Cash payments from the business
- Cash receipts to the business
- Closing and opening bank balances for the month

A cash-flow forecast shows the cycle of the business. Income and expenditure are ideally timed to match each other.

It is important to note that cash inflows generally lag behind outflows of cash from the business. Therefore, any imbalances can be identified through the use of a cash-flow forecast.

**Activity 30 – Explain why cash flow forecasting is important to a business.**

## How to Structure a Cash-Flow Forecast

Cash-flow forecasts are often set out with different columns for each month of the year. The cash-flow forecast is also known as the cash budget. It shows three distinct sets of figures. These include:

- Payments
- Receipts
- Monthly cash-flow for the month and the bank balance at the beginning of and end of each month

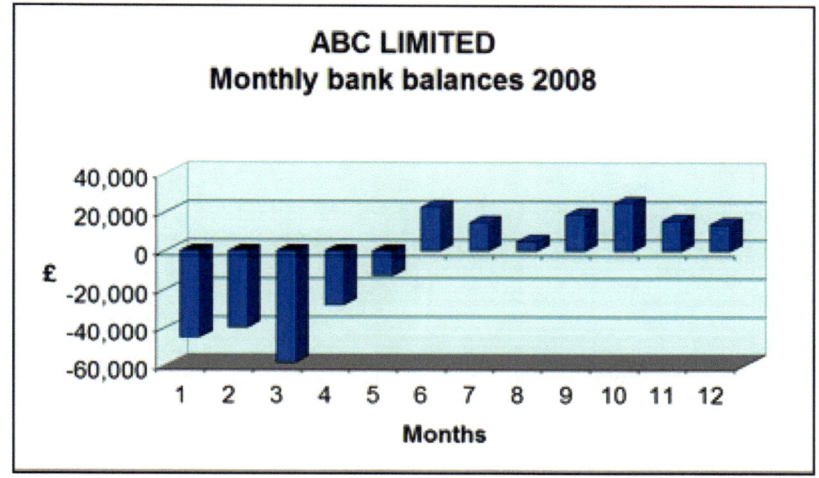

The cash-flow forecast shows the list of payments made out of the bank account. These include materials, miscellaneous expenses, wages and stock.

The receipts in the cash-flow forecast, show the list of items which have been paid into the bank account of the business. These include loans, sales and grants.

The cash-flow of the business is the difference between the total monthly receipts and the total monthly payments. Cash-flow forecasts can be calculated through the use of computer spreadsheets and 'what-if' scenarios.

Below is a more detailed breakdown of a cash flow forecast:

|  | A                B | D | E | F | G | H | I | J |
|---|---|---|---|---|---|---|---|---|
| 1 | ABC Photography | | | | | | | |
| 2 | Cashflow Forecast | | | | | | | |
| 3 | | January | February | March | April | May | June | Totals |
| 4 | Summary | | | | | | | |
| 5 | Beginning Cash Balance | 25,000 | 21,525 | 23,600 | 24,150 | 23,560 | 22,110 | |
| 6 | Sources | 7,250 | 11,200 | 13,500 | 9,450 | 7,500 | 10,500 | 59,400 |
| 7 | Uses | 10,725 | 9,125 | 12,950 | 10,040 | 8,950 | 9,850 | 61,640 |
| 8 | Net Change in Cash | (3,475) | 2,075 | 550 | (590) | (1,450) | 650 | (2,240) |
| 9 | Ending Cash Balance | 21,525 | 23,600 | 24,150 | 23,560 | 22,110 | 22,760 | |
| 10 | | | | | | | | |
| 11 | Sources of Cash | | | | | | | |
| 12 | Events - Deposits | 1,500 | 3,000 | 3,000 | 1,500 | 1,500 | 3,000 | 13,500 |
| 13 | Events - Final payments | 1,500 | 4,500 | 7,500 | 4,500 | 3,000 | 4,500 | 25,500 |
| 14 | Albums - Deposits | - | 500 | 1,000 | 500 | 1,000 | 1,500 | 4,500 |
| 15 | Albums - Final payments | 2,500 | 1,000 | | 500 | 1,000 | 500 | 5,500 |
| 16 | Other shooting revenue | 1,000 | 1,200 | 750 | 1,000 | 500 | 500 | 4,950 |
| 17 | Reprint revenue | 500 | 750 | 1,000 | 1,200 | 250 | 250 | 3,950 |
| 18 | Other | 250 | 250 | 250 | 250 | 250 | 250 | 1,500 |
| 19 | Total Sources of Cash | 7,250 | 11,200 | 13,500 | 9,450 | 7,500 | 10,500 | 59,400 |
| 20 | | | | | | | | |
| 21 | Uses of Cash | | | | | | | |
| 22 | Image processing | 450 | 450 | 1,350 | 2,250 | 1,350 | 900 | 6,750 |
| 23 | Printing costs | 100 | 150 | 200 | 240 | 50 | 50 | 790 |
| 24 | Album - Deposits | - | 125 | 250 | 125 | 250 | 375 | 1,125 |
| 25 | Album - Final payments | 625 | 250 | - | 125 | 250 | 125 | 1,375 |
| 26 | Salary & benefits, including med ins | 6,000 | 6,000 | 6,000 | 6,000 | 6,000 | 6,000 | 36,000 |
| 27 | Rent, occupancy & office expenses | 950 | 950 | 950 | 950 | 950 | 950 | 5,700 |
| 28 | Non-recurring expenses (ins, taxes) | 2,500 | 450 | 1,200 | - | - | 1,200 | 5,350 |
| 29 | New equipment | 100 | 750 | 3,000 | 350 | 100 | 250 | 4,550 |
| 30 | Total Uses of Cash | 10,725 | 9,125 | 12,950 | 10,040 | 8,950 | 9,850 | 61,640 |

**How to enter data on a cash-flow projection**

The cash-flow statement and the cash-flow forecast are similar in nature. The only difference between the two is that the statement shows the actual values, and the forecasts show the predicted values.

The following is a list of the data that can be found in a cash-flow projection:

- Cash in Hand
- Income
- Outgoings
- Total Cash Receipts
- Total Cash Available
- Total Cash Paid Out
- Cash Position

Cash-flow forecasts reflect any figures that are due to be received or paid out by the business.

They are a useful tool in establishing estimates for the business.

**Topic 2.2 - Financial Planning**

**Learning Outcome**

The aim of this section is for students to understand the following:

- Sales Forecasting
- Sales, revenue and cost
- Break Even
- Budgets
- Financial Planning
- Sales Forecasting

The purpose of a sales forecast is for management to estimate the number of sales that their product or service will make in the future. An organisation needs to look into the future to plan the launch of new products, investments, and if they need to withdraw certain products.

Management make key decisions from sales forecasting including:

- Workforce planning – how many staff they need and the skills base they require
- Marketing – promotion and mix
- Production capacity to meet anticipated demand
- Management of stocks

Getting the sales forecasting wrong can have severe consequences to an organisation, costing time, money and resources.

Factors which can affect sales forecasting are:

- Consumer trends – whatever is the latest fashion at the time
- Economic variables – recession or recovery
- Competitors – e.g. Aldi supermarket has taken sales away from established supermarkets such as Tesco, Morrison's and Asda

These factors make sales forecasting difficult as all businesses operate in a dynamic market where sales are not guaranteed.

**Sales, revenue and costs**

Every business must use its financial resources effectively in order to conduct its activities successfully. These financial resources could come from a range of sources, but whatever the source, it must be used with due care as it is always limited.

When a business uses capital to purchase fixed assets, this is called capital expenditure.

The retained profits are financial resources that the business generates as a direct result of its profitability; these are called retained profits.

There is also another source of business funding which is referred to as working capital. This is used for the day-to-day running of the business including bill payments, stock purchases, wage payments and others.

There are various types of costs which the business accrues in the course of performing its activities. These include:

- Fixed costs
- Variable costs

Fixed costs are incurred by the business as a result of the business operations. Regardless of the level and type of business activity, fixed costs are standard and fixed.

Typical examples of fixed costs include: employees' wages, utility bills, rent, and insurance. These costs can increase to reflect the rise in prices of the above mentioned for any reason, including inflation.

Variable costs are not constant, and increase or decrease as a direct result of the output levels for the business and on factors external to the business and beyond your control.

There is direct a proportional relationship between variable costs and output. Hence with an increase in the level of production of the goods and service, the higher the variable costs will be.

Variable costs = Total costs – fixed costs

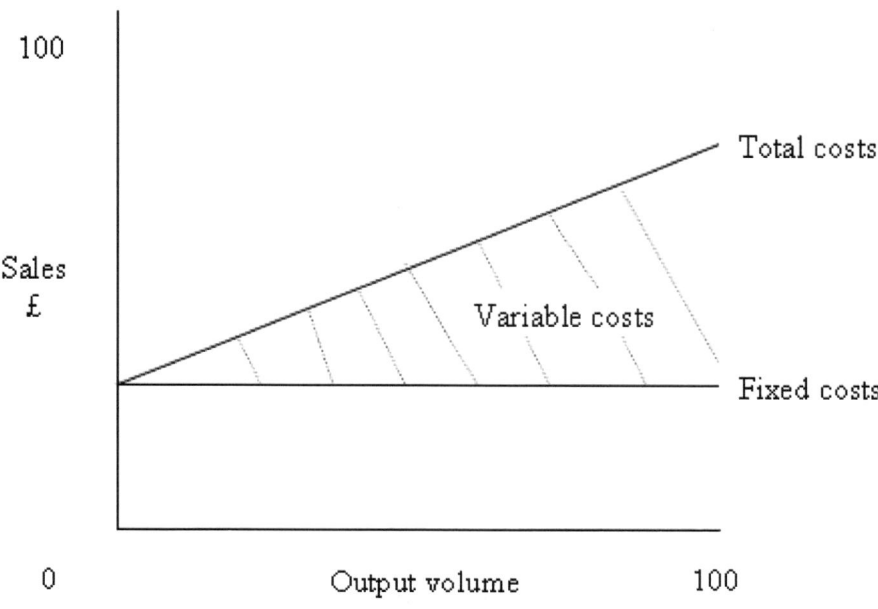

## Total and Average Costs

The total cost of a business is the sum total of both the fixed and variable costs which the business accrues as a direct result of its operation. The average cost is the cost per unit of production. In other words:

$$\text{Average costs} = \frac{\text{Total costs}}{\text{Output}}$$

## Activity 31 – Why do you think a business would be interested in its average cost?

**Direct and Indirect Costs**

Direct costs are defined as the variable costs of the business which directly relate to the output level of production.

Indirect costs are the fixed costs which are accrued by the business that are spread across the business in different areas. For example, the rent is paid by the business for the use of all departments involved in production. It is essential and cannot be categorised as a variable cost which changes.

**Price, Total Revenue and Profit**

The calculation of price

A product's price is never random. In order to set the price of any product or service, the following factors need to be considered:

- Business Costs – direct, indirect, fixed and variable cost
- Competitor prices – these could be lower and hence the business must be sensible in setting its price to attract clients

This process of setting the price of goods and services is known as the pricing policy. New businesses need to realise the importance of pricing policy.

- Firstly, the competition in the market among established leaders makes it difficult for a new business to set its price.
- Secondly, start-up costs will be high as it is a new business. It may not have the access to benefits of large scale production.
- It would like its business service and product to gain maximum exposure at a relatively early stage. Therefore, it needs to be cautious with its pricing policy.

**How to calculate the business revenue**

Business revenue is the amount of profit which the business makes from its daily activities and its efforts to sell products and services to its respective market.

The price per unit of the product is multiplied by the number of units of the products sold:

Sales revenue = average price × volume of goods sold

As the business strives for growth, it would need to consider various ways to increase its revenue. These include:

- Increasing the average price per unit of product
- Increasing the volume of the products on the market

**Calculation of profit**

Profit = Total revenue - Total costs

The gross profit of a business is the total amount it makes before the deduction of any tax.

Operating profit of a business refers to the deduction of overhead costs from the total gross profits. These overheads include the business' fixed costs.

The business pre-tax profits are defined as the profit derived after the major one-off costs have been deducted from the operating profit.

The net profit of the business is the actual profit of the business which has been deducted of tax. Once corporation tax has been deducted, this is the level of profit left available for distribution to shareholders. It is also from this that retained profits are derived. These are ploughed back to be invested in the business.

The higher the profits of a business the more attractive it is to investors and the shareholders. The level of profit reflects the performance of the business and how effective the operating strategies and plans have been.

There is a strong relationship between profits, revenue, price and cost: profits are generated when revenues are high, as a result of good performance of the business. The higher the price in relation to the volume, the higher will be the revenue and hence the profits. The costs need to be kept to a minimum in order to produce more and generate the maximum returns.

However, in the case when the output costs, as a direct result of an increase in revenue, is equal to or exceeds the revenue generated, then there would be no profit made from the business. The higher the prices are in direct relation to the revenue.

Businesses always endeavour to minimise costs and create the most favourable opportunities for profit maximisation.

**Self-assessment questions:**

1) Explain the various methods of calculation of costs, revenues and profits.
2) What are the differences between fixed, variable and total costs?
3) Discuss the relationship between price, total revenue and profits.

**Break-even**

**Introduction**

In this section we will look at the concepts of:

- Contribution per unit
- Contribution
- Break-even analysis

We will also look at the importance of how contribution relates to price and profit is also covered. Break-even analysis is used by businesses to reveal its revenues in relation to its costs at different levels of demand and output.

We will also analyse the changing variables that are involved in determining revenues and cost levels and the effects that such variable can have on the business activities.

Inasmuch as the concepts in this section are very beneficial to the business, it must be clearly understood that these concepts also have their limitations and strengths. These are clearly analysed in this unit.

**Contribution and Contribution per Unit**

Contribution = Sales revenue - Variable costs

The contribution is the difference between the income which is generated from the sales revenue and the variable costs that were used to produce the revenue-making goods and services.

Once the variable costs have been deducted, the outstanding cost left is the fixed overhead costs. We can say that the fixed cost overheads are paid for by the contribution because the contribution is what remains after a deduction of only variable costs has been made.

The contribution per unit is the amount that every single unit of produced goods will generate after the variable costs have been deducted and the fixed overheads can be taken care of. Profit can only be generated after the costs have been taken care of.

When a toyshop buys teddy bears from its supplier for £4.20 and sells them in its shop at £6.40, then the contribution per unit of each teddy bear is £2.20 (£6.40 - £4.20 = £2.20).

The following factors can affect the contribution per unit:

- Selling Price – the higher the selling price of the good or service, the greater the contribution per unit and vice versa. When this is high, the overhead costs can be taken care of more effectively including the rent or mortgage repayment for the business and utility bills
- Variable costs – a reduction in the outgoings of the business will inversely affect the contribution per unit. In other words, as the business finds cost-effective ways to produce its goods and services, the higher will be the contribution per unit available to the business

Businesses can reduce variable costs by outsourcing to cost-effective and specialist contractors, switching to more affordable suppliers who provide similar or better quality of the same resources for production; minimising unnecessary expenses which the business accumulates without productive reasons.

There is a link between the pricing, profit and contribution. Profit can only be generated after the contribution has covered the fixed overheads costs. Costs must be considered when setting process. When the cost is high, the set price is high, otherwise it will result in the high costs outweighing the profit potential of the goods or services.

As long as the selling price can outweigh the cost of production while the costs are kept to the very minimum, the contribution will be high.

With increased contributions per unit, fixed cost and variable costs are minimised and the profit which the business generates increases in proportion to the sales revenue which should exceed the total costs.

Businesses use contribution to determine whether the goods they produce are contributing in any way to offset the variable costs they incur.

The effect of this for the business is that it enables the business to set its prices based on what it actually spends on production of the same goods, instead of overstating the price to include the fixed costs of the business. Therefore products with a high contribution per unit will help to offset the fixed costs.

**Contribution and break-even**

Contribution is also closely linked to break-even. As a business increases its production, it is expected that every individual product makes a positive contribution to the business. In effect this would mean that the products are covering the fixed costs quicker, and fewer of them have to be made before the break-even point is reached.

Since the business is increasing its production range, it is anticipated that the revenue of sales will be high. As the sales revenue rises and the contribution per unit rises, the fixed overhead costs will be paid off faster.

For new business start-ups, the fixed overheads costs tend to be relatively high. However, as the sales revenue rises with contribution per unit, it will in effect pay off the fixed costs faster and result in the making of business profits.

The point at which the contribution per unit equals and begins to exceed the fixed cost overhead is known as the break-even point. It can be calculated as:

$$\text{Break-even point} = \frac{\text{Fixed costs}}{\text{Contribution (per unit)}}$$

For example, a sandwich business has fixed costs of £25,000 and contribution per unit of £1. The break-even point of the business will be:

$$\frac{£25,000}{£1} = 25000 \text{ units}$$

From this calculation, the business will break-even when 25000 units have been produced and sold by the business, assuming no hidden or extra costs.

## How to Calculate Break-even Output and Construction of Break-even Charts

### Break even charts

Look at the break-even chart below which shows a diagrammatic representation of the analysis and more in-depth information on the costs and revenue at all levels of output and demand. Any diagrammatic representation would require the following:

- Revenues
- Output
- Costs

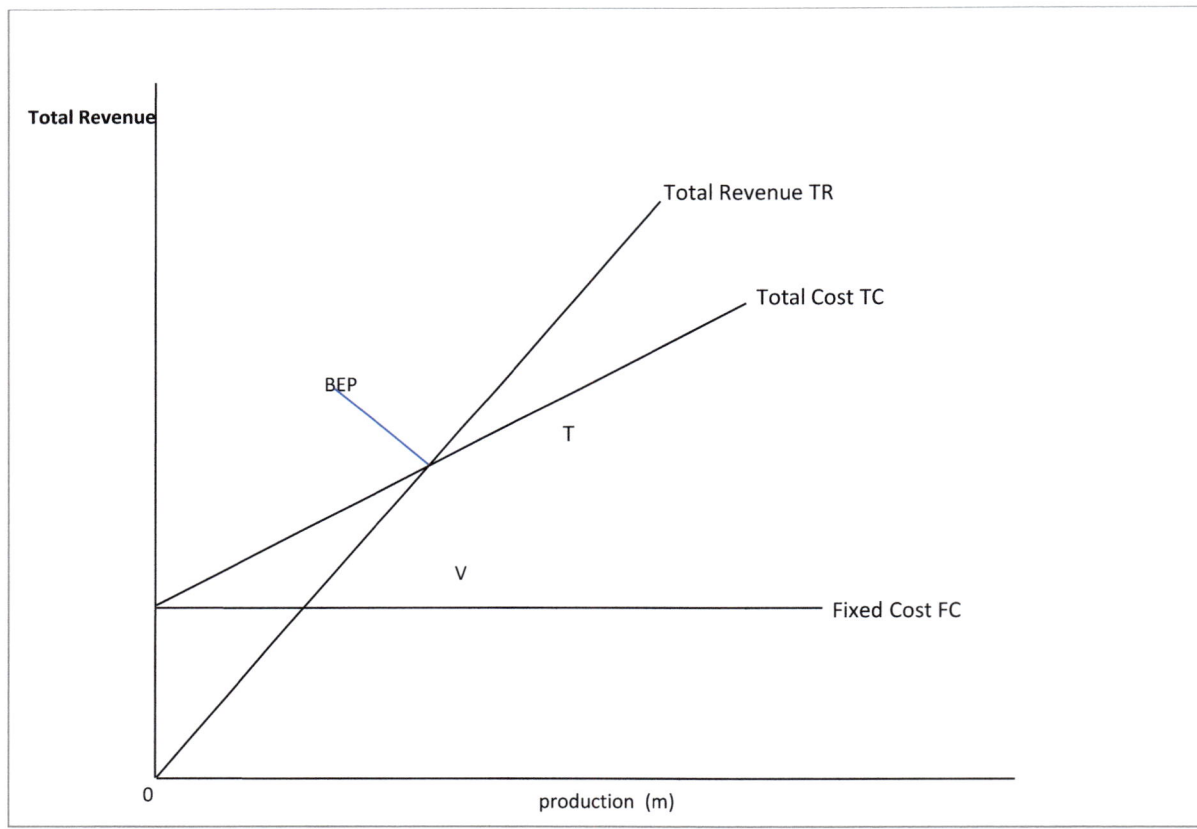

From the above diagram, the break-even point (BEP) is the point at which the total revenue (TR) line crosses the total cost line (TC).

Let us look at a practical application of the break-even analysis:

| Quantity of Produced Units | Fixed Costs (FC) | Variable Costs (VC) @ £3 per unit | Total Costs (TC) = FC + VC |
|---|---|---|---|
| 0 | 3000 | 0 | 3000 |
| 500 | 3000 | 1500 | 4500 |
| 1000 | 3000 | 3000 | 6000 |
| 1500 | 3000 | 4500 | 7500 |

Let us assume the goods were sold at a unit price £4.50. Therefore:

| Output | Total Revenue (output x unit price) |
|---|---|
| 0 | 0 |
| 500 | 2250 |
| 1000 | 4500 |
| 1500 | 6750 |

When the break-even chart is plotted based on the above information, then the break-even point (BEP) can be obtained.

There is an area of profit and loss in the BEP chart which shows the profit or loss that can be made. Any level of production of output that is above the break-even point leads to profits. On the contrary, any area that falls below the break-even point leads to making potential losses.

This is illustrated below:

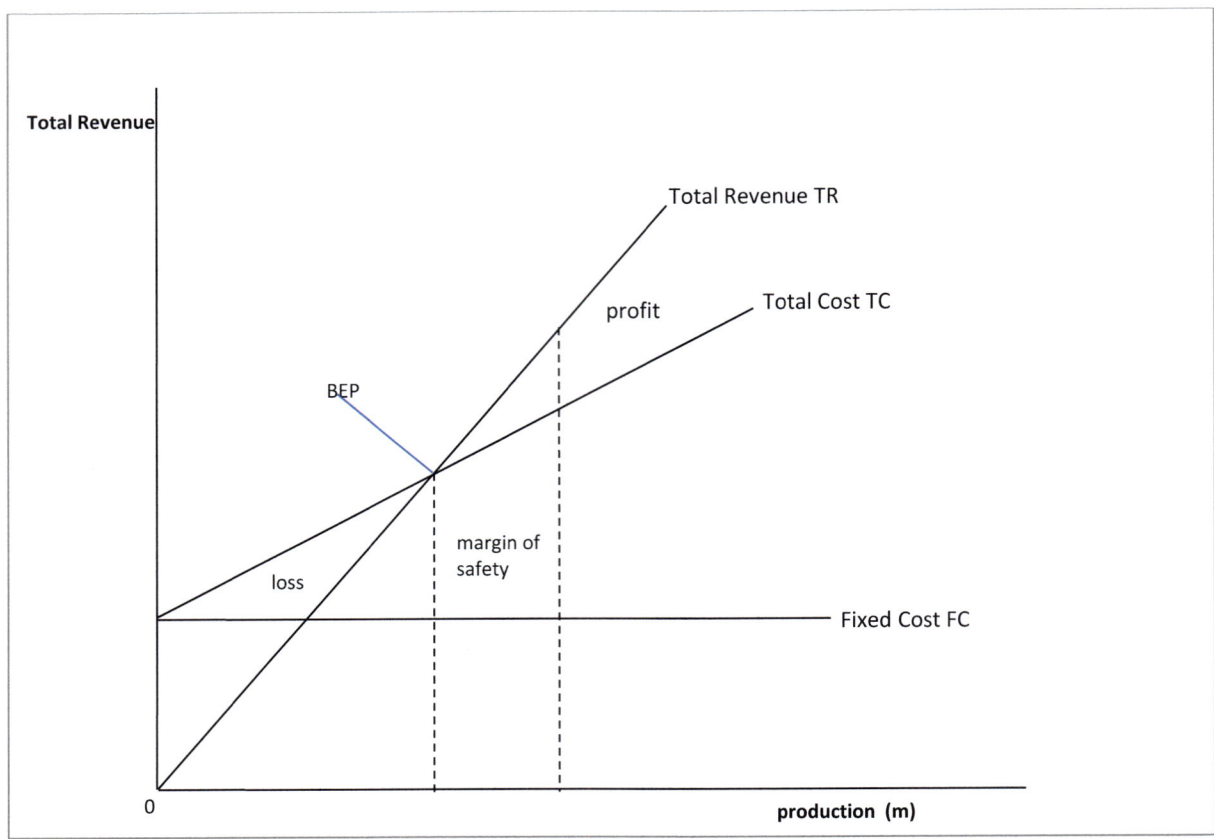

The area shown by the margin of safety is the total revenue and total current output. Hence this reflects the current output level at any point on the total revenue line. This difference between the point on the total revenue line and the break-even point is the margin of safety.

The implication of the margin of safety for the business is that it reflects the level of fall in demand for a product that can be experienced before it leads to business losses.

Hence when this is understood by the business, it realises the need for a wide safety margin which occurs through creating greater gaps between the current sales and break-even point.

## Analysing changing variables and their effects

### Budget plan

The effects of changes in the variables that affect the businesses profit and loss should be shown in its budget plan. This plan proposes financial targets including the level of sales and production for a defined time period. It has the benefit of ensuring continued business focus to facilitate efficient planning and control.

### Direct costs

The changes in this type of variable tend to affect the variable cost of the business, and in effect, the total cost. It has several effects when the total revenue crosses the total cost line including:

- Altering the break-even line
- Change in the margin of safety
- Change in the profit and loss areas
- Changes to the fixed costs due to changes in overhead costs

### Numerical calculation

There are also numerical calculations which are involved in executing the budget action plan and helping the business attain its targets. It could be calculating the elasticity of prices which measures the impact of price changes on the demand for the product. Here is how to determine the price elasticity:

$$\text{Price elasticity} = \frac{\text{The percentage change in quantity demanded}}{\text{The percentage change in price}}$$

For example, assume a business suffers from a 30% fall in demand for increasing its prices by 10%.

Using the above formula you will see that the price elasticity and responsiveness for the product demand to any slight change in price will be -3.

Hence demand for the product will change by 3% for every 1% price change. This is a negative relationship because price rises normally lead to levels of demand dropping and vice versa.

Through the use of trial and error, a business can also find the effect of prices on the demand for its products.

**Changing overheads**

The changes in this type of variable tend to affect the fixed cost and total cost lines of the business. In effect, total revenue crosses the total cost line at a different point. Furthermore, it causes:

- Changes in the margin of safety
- Shift of the fixed cost line due to changes in the overhead costs which is a fixed cost
- Alterations to the break-even line
- Changes in the profit and loss areas

**Activity 32 – How can a business act to reduce its overheads?**

**Target profit levels of activity**

When the amount of profit a business makes falls, it will need to seek to maintain the optimum revenue in order to sustain the best position for optimum profit.

To achieve this, the business must:

- Experience a fall in variable costs that are related with each level of output and causing the line of total cost to be reduced
- Experience an increase in the price of each product sold, thereby reducing the units sold prior to the total cost line actually intersecting with total revenue to create the break-even point
- Experience a fall in fixed costs to reduce the total cost

**Activity 33 – How might a business increase its revenue?**

**Pros and cons of Break-even analysis**

There are always benefits and drawbacks of any method of analysis. These are reflected in the following business areas:

- Consistency of the sale price - Throughout the life cycle of any given product, it is bound to experience fluctuations in price, depending on the market, consumers, raw material costs and many other factors. Unfortunately break-even analysis assumes that the price does not change

- External factors - These factors include macroeconomic indicators such as fluctuations in interest rate, inflation and several other factors. These tend to affect the costs of production incurred by the business, and as they vary, so do the business costs. Break-even analysis ignores these external factors

- Sales and production levels - Break-even analysis assumes that the level of production and sales are matched by each other. In reality, this is not always the case. This is not taken into consideration in the break-even analysis

- The behaviour of overheads and contribution - Contribution is very important in calculating the break-even point. However, it should be noted that there are fluctuations in contribution which could change through increases or decreases in production, which will lead to profit increases or decreases in a very short space of time. Furthermore, the behaviour of overheads or fixed costs can lead to enormous strain on the products as the contribution is greatly affected. These fixed costs can increase or decrease notwithstanding the output produced. This could be through changes in the rent prices or moving to a bigger complex to facilitate production. Such measures affect contribution per unit and inevitably will affect the break-even analysis calculation

**Self-assessment questions**

1) Explain why Break-even Analysis is an important tool in decision-making.
2) What is the importance of Contribution and Contribution per unit in the business?
3) Explain the methods of analysing changing variables and their effects.

**Budgets**

**Importance of Setting Budgets and Arising Problems**

A budget can be defined as the pattern of expenses and income that have been pre-agreed by a business which establishes its goals for costs and revenues over any given period of time in the future. Budgets have a number of functions:

- The adequate co-ordination of business activities
- Provision of a focus for the future for business
- They serve as a tool of motivation to exceed expectations
- Provision of analysis for the future
- They provide a basis for evaluating past and present business performance
- Essential communication in the formulation of business plans for the future

A business needs well-defined and feasible targets in order to set a budget. Senior managers throughout the business are often involved in the process of setting the budget; this enables proper co-ordination across the entire business. With a degree of flexibility in a budget plan, it enables the ability to modify and make necessary changes at short-notice to account for unprecedented events.

Problems in setting a budget include the following:

- Resource Allocation
- Planning
- Setting of Targets
- Reviewing and modifying of the budget
- Adequate co-ordination

**Income, Expenditure and Profit Budgets**

There are several types of budgets which are used by businesses, including:

- Sales budget
- Production budget
- Debtors and Creditors
- Purchases
- Cash
- Standard costing

These are all powerful tools that the business uses to determine sales figures, costs of raw materials to the business, assessment of anticipated inflow and outflow of money from the business.

**The Process of Setting a Budget**

Without the use of a budget, it is easy for any enterprise to run into problems that could have been avoided.  Several steps are taken when preparing a budget:

- The identification of objectives for the business and how to use the budget to achieve them
- Control measures need to be in place in order to co-ordinate the operations which the business embarks upon in order to accomplish its targets
- Provision of reliable and accurate information. This ensures that the plans in the budget are flawless, feasible and can be accomplished

**Budget Amendments and Completions**

Businesses need to be prepared to make amendments and adjustments to the budget when necessary, such as the introduction of new products or external changes over which the business has no control e.g. change of legislation.

This flexibility will ensure that there are minimal variances between the actual figures and what was prescribed in the budget.

To achieve short-term targets the budget is a very useful tool. It reveals crucial areas of income and cost which can be manipulated to achieve profit targets and control of expenditure.

Furthermore, the regular monitoring of the budget helps the business to constantly be ahead of its target and pursue activities that will strengthen the competitiveness of the business.

**Activity 34 – What do you think might happen to variable costs if budgets are not controlled?**

**Variance Analysis**

How to calculate and interpret favourable and adverse variances

A variance is the difference between the actual figures which the business obtains and the figures projected in the budget. Errors in budgetary calculations can lead to variances.

Variances should be detected and dealt with quickly to ensure that the business does not suffer and that no serious errors are made financially.

The use of statistical and accounting information is very useful in showing any budget variances.

Several types of variances are possible:

- Labour variance
- Overhead variance
- Sales Variance
- Profit variance

Each of these variances is caused by fluctuations in the price or the change in the level of volumes as outlined in the budget.

The difference between the positive and negative variances are the effect on the budget and business performance.

Positive variances reveal that business is performing better than expected. However negative variances show the opposite and reflect the poor performance of the business.

**Making Informed decisions Based on Variance Analysis**

Through the calculation of the different types of variance, businesses can make informed decisions about the direction of the company. The different ways to calculate these variances are examined below.

**Labour variances**

There are three methods of calculating labour variance:

- Labour efficiency variance
- Total labour cost variance
- Labour rate price variance

Labour efficiency variance is used to measure whether more or less labour is needed to produce a specified number of units. Depending on the level of expertise required and the complexity of the units.

$$(AH - BH) \times BR$$

AH is the actual number of hours. The budgeted wage rate is BR and BH is the budgeted hours in which the work should be completed.

Total labour cost variance shows the difference that exists between the anticipated cost of direct labour and the actual cost of the direct labour. In other words,

$$(AR \times AH) - (BR \times BH)$$

AR is the actual wage rate and AH is the actual number of hours. The budgeted wage rate is BR and BH is the budgeted hours in which the work should be completed.

Labour rate price variance is the variance between the wage rate which was expected and the actual amount which was paid. In this case

$$(AR-BR) \times AH$$

AR is the actual wage rate and AH is the actual number of hours. The budgeted wage rate is BR.

**Overhead variances**

Overhead variances are calculated using the product of the budgeted variable overheads per unit and the actual production less the actual variable overhead cost. Hence:

(Budgeted variable overheads per unit x Actual production) – Actual variable overhead cost

The volume of overhead variances is calculated by:

(Budgeted quantity of input hours for actual production – Actual input hours)   x variable overhead rate

**Activity 35 – In your own words describe variance.**

**Material variance**

This type of variance examines the total cost of materials against the budgeted costs of material in the business, so:

$$(AQ \times AC) - (BQ \times BC)$$

AQ is the actual quantity

AC is the actual cost.

BQ is the budgeted quantity

BC is the budgeted cost

For example, a business uses 800 units at £8, giving a total of £6400. It had budgeted to use 860 units at £7 with a total cost of £6020. Therefore:

$$(£8 \times 800) - (£7 \times 860) = £6400 - £6020$$

$$\text{Adverse variance} = £380$$

For direct materials the calculation of price variance is

$$(AC - BC) \times AQ$$

AQ is the actual quantity and AC is the actual cost. BC is the budgeted cost.

For example:

$$(£8 - £7) \times 800) = £1 \times 800$$

$$\text{Adverse variance} = £800$$

To calculate the variance on the materials which are used, the equation is

$$(AQ - BQ) \times BC$$

AQ is the actual quantity and BQ is the budget quantity. BC is the budgeted cost.

For example:

$$(800 - 860) \times £7 = -60 \times £7$$

$$\text{Favourable variance} = -£420$$

**Sales variance**

This can be calculated on the sales variance of the price or the sales variance of the volume. The impact of either of these two variances on the sale can be determined using the formula:

$$\text{Sales revenue variance} = (AP \times AQ) - (BP \times BQ)$$

Where AQ is the actual quantity which is sold and AP is the actual price per unit. The budget price anticipated is BP and the budget quantity that is sold is BQ

An example of this is shown below:

A clothing shop budgets to sell 200,000 units of clothes but instead sells 180,000 units. It was expected that the price for every unit of clothing would be £5 but instead this was £4.50.

The revenue from sales was budgeted at £1000,000 but the actual sales revenue was £810,000. There was a variance in the sales revenue due to both a lower quantity sold and a lower actual sales price. Therefore:

$$Sales\ revenue\ variance = (AP \times AQ) - (BP \times BQ)$$

$$= (£4.5 \times 180,000) - (£5 \times 200,000)$$

$$= £810000 - £1000000$$

$$= -£190000$$

Price variance uses:

$$Price\ variance = (AP - BP) \times AQ$$

Based on the above example this will be:

$$(£4.50 - £5) \times 180000 = £90000$$

Quantity or volume variance uses:

$$Quantity\ variance = (AQ - BQ) \times BP$$

Based on the above example this will be:

$$(180000 - 200000) \times £5 = -£100000$$

It should be noted that the price variance was of a much lesser significance than the volume variance. The volume variance contributed £100,000 significantly more in comparison to the price variance that contributed £90,000.

**The Difficulties of Budgeting**

There are several types of budgeting which businesses can use to formulate plans to grow and develop the business. These include:

- Zero budgeting - Zero budgets set the business budget at zero. It is very useful in enhancing the business co-ordination and to enhance the activities of the business
- Historical budgeting - historical budgets use the figures from the previous year in setting the budget. It takes into account the revenues and costs figures and uses this to establish the budget figures for the following year
- Flexible budgeting - Flexible budgeting is used to amend any circumstances that could change the business focus. Whatever might cause the business to re-evaluate its activities and action plans can be taken into account for by the flexible budget

**Benefits and drawbacks**

There are several benefits of budgeting:

- Budgets are useful in the co-ordination of departmental budgets to get an instant picture of the overall business
- Budgets are used to monitor and control costs. This is because any expenses have to be approved by the person who is responsible for executing the budget
- The motivation of the business has a strong link to the budget

The drawbacks of budgeting:

- There may be the need to take short-term actions to be within the budget in the event that the information which is provided in the budget is not accurate
- There can be power struggles within the business by those who are more favourably placed to influence the budget decisions than other less favoured work colleagues and counterparts who have little or no influence in the business

**Self-assessment questions**

1) What is the importance of setting budgets and the arising problems?
2) Distinguish between income, expenditure and profit budgets
3) Highlight the processes of setting a budget
4) What are budget amendments and completions?
5) Explain the different processes involved in managing a business
6) Highlight the importance of using budgets
7) What are variables? Distinguish between favourable and adverse variances
8) Which methods are used by businesses to make informed decision-making based on the analysis of variance?

**Topic 2.3 - Managing Finance**

**Learning Outcome**

The aim of this section is for students to understand the following:

- Profit
- Liquidity
- Business Failure

**Profit**

The aim of a business is to generate profit as a return or reward for the organisation and to measure the organisations success.

Profit can be described as the revenue from the sale of a service or a product less the costs, whereas cash is the actual money received for the service or product.

A business measures cash by means of a cash flow account and profit using various accounting ratio measures.

There are different ways in which an organisation can measure profit:

- Gross profit – is the total revenue minus the cost of sales
- Gross profit = revenue – cost of sales
- Operating profit – is gross profit minus other operating expenses
- Operating profit = gross profit – other operating expenses
- Net profit – is what is left over after all costs have been taken from sales revenue
- Net profit = operating profit – interest

**Gross Profit Margin**

This is an accounting ratio to assess an organisation's financial health by measuring the proportion of revenue left after accounting for the cost of sales. The direct costs involved with the business.

The ratio used is as follows and is shown as a percentage.

$$\text{Gross Profit Margin} = \frac{\text{Gross Profit}}{\text{Revenue}} \times 100$$

**Operating Profit Margin**

This is an accounting measure of what proportion of revenue is remaining before tax or any indirect costs, but after payment of variable costs. A good operating margin means the organisation has a low financial risk, as it is able to pay its fixed costs.

The ratio used is as follows and is shown as a percentage.

$$\text{Operating Profit Margin} = \frac{\text{Operating Profit}}{\text{Revenue}} \times 100$$

**Net Profit Margins**

The net profit margin can be a useful and simple method of measuring the performance of a business.

It is part of ratio analysis and reflects the level of profit. The net profit ratio examines the profit when overhead expenses have been deducted and also takes into account the turnover of the business.

The ratio used is as follows and is shown as a percentage.

$$\text{Net profit margin} = \frac{\text{Net profit}}{\text{Revenue}} \times 100$$

**Methods of Improving Profits and Profitability**

There are several ways for businesses to improve profits and profitability.

Businesses always strive to reduce their overall costs; this is because the higher the business costs; the lower will be the profit to the business.

There are several types of profit including:

- Gross profit
- Net profit
- Retained profit
- Disposable profit

Whichever type of profit you consider, the idea of profitability is to minimise the expenses of the business, which in turn leads to generation of higher profits in return.

In reducing business costs, all aspects of the costs of the business must be accounted for. These include everything from fixed costs to variable costs.

Inflation and rises in prices of products can affect the profits and profitability of the business.

Lower prices generally increase demand for products, and there is more profit made by the business. The converse effect applies when prices rise.

Businesses can try to improve their profitability through reducing their costs such as switching suppliers or changing methods of distribution.

**Differentiating between Cash and Profit**

Cash and profit are sometimes conflated as having the same implications on the business; this is not the case, however.

Cash is the ability of the business to cover its expenses in a timely manner. It could be obtained from cash in-flows, cheques and cash, and it is reduced by cash out-flows.

When cash is built up by a business, there is a strong reserve in case of emergency, which ensures the viability of the business.

Note that when we refer to cash, we are not talking about physical money, but cash reserves in a bank account.

Profit is the made through business cash in-flows. When the expenses incurred by the business are deducted from the sales revenue, then the remainder is the profit of the business. It is calculated often monthly, quarterly or annually.

Money borrowing, long-term deposits, and money which customers owe can eventually become business profit. This is because they are not instantly available to the business.

## Activity 36 – What is profitability and what factors can affect it?

**Self-assessment questions**

1) Explain the methods of measurement and increase of profit in a business.

2) How does a business analyse the net profit margins?

3) What are the implications of the return on capital for the business?

**Liquidity**

Organisations present a statement of their financial position or a balance sheet at a given date normally at the end of a financial year. This presents the assets, the liabilities and the equity of the business at that time. This is a snapshot of the businesses financial health.

The statement of financial position is presented as follows:

Non-current assets + Current assets – Current liabilities – non-current liabilities = Net assets

**Liquidity ratios**

Liquidity ratios are used to measure the ability of the firm to meet its daily expenses by comparing the current liabilities and assets of the business. Such comparisons are important in assessing if the business is viable in the short term.

The current ratio and acid test ratio are the two frequently used liquidity tests.

The current ratio is presented as follows:

$$\text{Current ratio} = \frac{\text{Current Assets}}{\text{Current Liabilities}}$$

The acid test ratio is presented as follows:

Acid test ratio is the difference between the current assets and inventories expressed as a ratio to the current liabilities. That is:

$$\text{Acid test ratio} = \frac{\text{(Current assets – Inventory)}}{\text{Current liabilities}}$$

Hence at XYZ plc, the acid test ratio is:

$$\text{Acid test ratio} \;=\; \frac{(280 - 40)}{220}$$

$$\text{Acid test ratio} \;=\; \frac{240}{220}$$

$$\text{Acid test ratio} = 1{:}1.09$$

Therefore, for every £1 of current liabilities, it has £1.09 of current assets which excludes the inventories.

**Business Failure**

Starting up a new business is a process that is full of risks. From location, to investor needs, to building a client-base and finance, are mitigating factors that show the levels of risks which are involved in business start-ups.

The cash-flow of a new business will generally differ significantly from that of a well-established business. Start-ups can be aided in this regard, however, by banks and financial institutions through loans, overdrafts and other facilities.

Getting access to finance is not always easy, however, and is particularly problematic for businesses in more risky sectors, or of a type that the bank might consider risky. For instance, limited companies are given preference over sole traders.

Intense competition in the market can create strong barriers for new businesses. New businesses need to develop a strong and loyal customer base, and this only happens over time and is only possible when the business proves that it is worthy of becoming a player in the market and a force to be reckoned with in business.

Location is very important and can make or break a new enterprise. The right location creates the right marketing and attraction factors for the business.

Furthermore, location enhances the image and exposure of the business. It is futile to enter a competitive market and fail to make attempts to be recognised. The results of such behaviour lead to repeated failures in the business.

**Reasons for failure of business Start-ups**

New businesses are frequently faced with changes in the market which have a direct impact on its performance. The change in costs of the business and levels of demand for the products are important factors in the failure of businesses. There are external factors than can affect a new business such as economic recession, the strengthening of the pound sterling against other currencies or a reduction in export demand due to competition or trade restrictions.

The internal factors can include poor management efficiency where the business is unable to react quickly enough to changes, lack of marketing of product or service which fails to attract and retain customers and failure to innovate new products in an evolving market.

Several factors can also lead to the success or failure of the business including:

- Changes in lifestyle
- Advertising levels
- Income of the customer base
- Population changes
- Implications of laws on the business
- Price of the product
- Skills of competitors

In addition to the above, every business needs reliable suppliers, not just the cheapest. However, when businesses are new or in a new market it is usually trial and error to find out who are the best suppliers. Bad suppliers will have a negative impact on the business. They create unnecessary delays and inevitably lead to a rise in the prices of the products.

**Activity 37 – What effect might a poor supplier have on your customers, and therefore on your business?**

**Self-assessment questions**

1) Describe the aims and objectives of business start-ups.

2) Highlight the strengths and weaknesses of business ideas or plans.

3) What are the risks involved with business start-ups?

4) Discuss the reasons for failure of business start-ups.

**Topic 2.4 - Resource Management**

**Learning Outcome**

The aim of this section is for students to understand the following:

- Production, productivity and efficiency
- Capacity Utilisation
- Stock Control
- Quality Management

## Production, Productivity and Efficiency

Operational targets are the objectives which are set by the business which can be achieved and surpassed; failure to do so can have serious repercussions for the business.

The components of operational targets include:

- Capacity utilisation - Capacity utilisation is a vital component of operations target. It is the actual amount of capacity that a business uses in the current period
- Quality - Quality standards are another aspect of operations targets that are very important to the business. Without the guarantee of high quality standard, a business will lose potential customers and could also be in breach of government legislation on quality standards
- Costs - Costs which a business incurs can be fixed or variable. Such costs especially fixed costs are not directly related to the levels of production. However, it needs to be evenly distributed among the units produced. Therefore the contribution made by each unit is high when the capacity utilisation is at a low level. With an increase in capacity utilisation, there is a reduction in contribution necessary per unit

**Activity 38 – Why do you think operational targets can help a business?**

**Methods of Production**

Production is where the business converts the input into an output for products or services which a customer has ordered. The methods of production can be split into:

- Job production – this is where orders are created for 'one off' or 'bespoke' customers. The size of the order can be small, such as a dress for a customer, to a much larger order, for example, a new sports stadium. A job production order is specialised with skilled employees to meet the exact specification for the customer order. This type of production is expensive and often used by small businesses. The lead time can be lengthy as specialist resources, equipment and skilled labour are required

- Batch production – is where customer orders are used in small and large batches. This production process is used by organisations that have different variations of the same product such as a car tyre manufacturer or a fast food caterer for the production of ready meals

- Flow production – this is where products are made in high volumes in a continuous flow from one production task to the next. The individual tasks are repetitive for employees and often completed by machines or robots. The aim of this production is speed without the loss of quality. For example a car manufacturer

- Cell production – is where the production line is split into a number of sections, each with a worker group known as a cell. Each cell takes responsibility for their area and is skilled in a number of tasks for job rotation purposes. The advantages are worker commitment for the completed task, improved team working and quality improvement of product

**Capacity Utilisation**

**How to Calculate and Manage Capacity Utilisation**

Capacity utilisation is a measure of current output against the maximum possible output.

$$\frac{\text{Current output}}{\text{Maximum output}} \quad x \quad 100$$

The maximum output is determined by a number of factors including the available labour, buildings and machinery, available capital, available raw materials etc.

When a business is working at 100% capacity utilisation, it is producing as much as it is capable of producing; in practice it will be rare to operate at 100% capacity utilisation. For example, if a business has a maximum possible output of 125,000 units per week and is currently producing 84,000 units per week, then capacity utilisation will be:

$$\frac{84000}{125000} \quad x \quad 100 \quad = \quad 67\%$$

To put it another way, the business is operating at 33% below its full capacity.

Managing capacity utilisation occurs through changes in the capacity. This could occur through changes in the levels of demand for products over a period of time. This will lead the business to:

- Rationalisation which increases efficiency and cuts capacity to raise the percentage utilisation
- Sell-off machinery or renting where necessary to reduce fixed costs
- Redundancy and reduction of working hours or shift transfers for employees

Advantages of operating at full capacity

- Optimisation of fixed assets in production
- Profit will be at maximum
- High demand for products and success in the business

Disadvantages of operating at full capacity

- Maintenance of machinery could be difficult
- Exceeding full capacity can result in too many customer demands which may not be met
- Leads to overworking of members of staff

**Activity 39 – Would you want your organisation to be operating at 100% capacity? Explain your answer.**

## Matching Production and Demand

With the optimum utilisation of capacity there tends to be a high level of demand for the products and services which the business has to offer. In order to match the levels of demand created by the full capacity utilisation, the business has options which include:

- Hiring seasonal workers
- Expansion of the business
- Making more work shifts and overtime for workers
- Subcontracting and outsourcing

A combination of the above tends to ensure that the business is able to match the demand for its products adequately. There are instances when the business capacity utilisation is lower than anticipated. This increases burdens on the fixed costs. To increase capacity utilisation then the business can:

- Reduce working hours
- Expand its client base
- Reduce its wage rates
- Downsize and rationalise

## Self-assessment questions

1) Define the term 'operations management'.
2) Explain the function of operational targets in business.
3) Discuss the ways in which businesses can match their production and demand.

**Stock Control**

Effective stock control involves carefully planning to ensure that the business does not run out of stock and lead to production stopping.

Stock Control Diagram

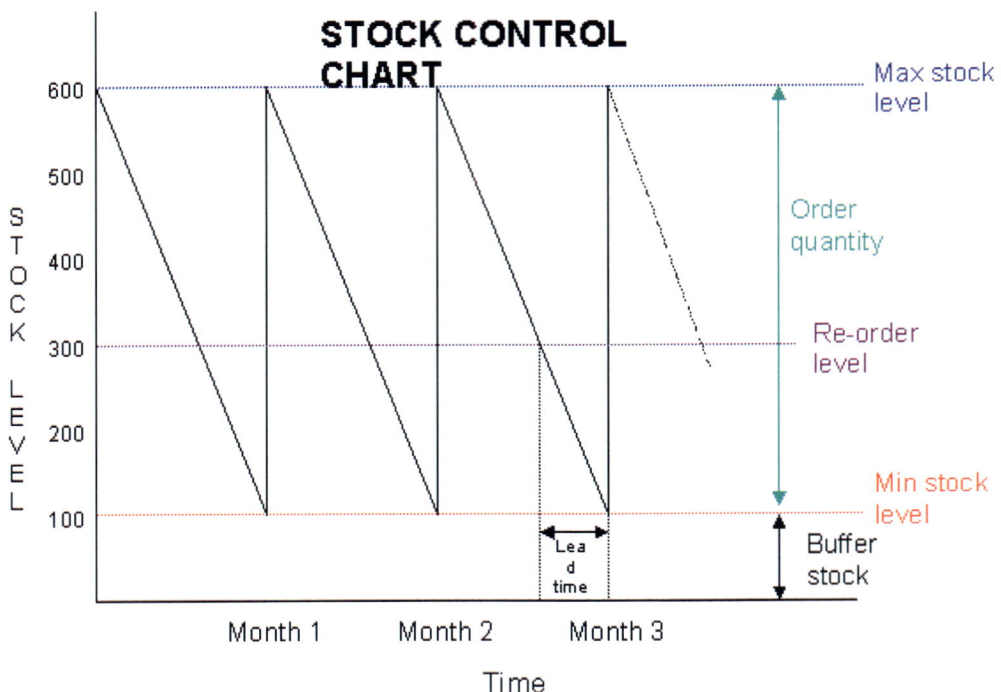

- Maximum stock level – this is the maximum an organisation does not want to hold in stock. This may be due to warehouse space or enough stock for order for the next month
- Re-order level – this is a trigger for the next stock order that needs to be placed. This new order should arrive before the stocks fall below the minimum order
- Lead time – is the time the stock takes to arrive at the organisation when the order has been placed with the supplier
- Minimum stock – the minimum amount of product the organisation would want to hold in stock
- Buffer stock – the amount of stock the organisation holds in the event of an unexpected order.

If a business has poor stock control it can mean it is unable to meet customer demand, complete orders on time or offer quality goods.

**Lean Production**

This is a Japanese approach to management that focuses on waste minimisation and the quality of the product. Lean production aims to make the business more efficient and cost effective. The approach is to remove all activities that do not add value to the production process: for example, holding stock, product faults, unnecessary movement of staff and products around the factory. One of the principles of lean production is 'just in time' management of stock.

## Just in Time (JIT) Management of Stock

This is where stock is ordered to meet specific orders with very little or no stock held at the organisation. Businesses that operate this way need very reliable suppliers who can provide and deliver products quickly.[1] So that production is continuous and deadlines can be met. This removes the need for storage facilities to hold stock and therefore can reduce costs. This can give the business a competitive advantage as their reduced costs can be passed onto the customer through price.

---

[1] It is interesting to note the impact of the Japanese tsunami of 2011 on the supply chain in this regard. As an example, see: http://businesstheory.com/reducing-risk-automotive-supply-chain-2/

**Quality Management**

**Introduction to Quality**

Producing a quality product or providing a quality service is vital to any business. Quality is a defining factor in the success of attracting high calibre customers, or in losing customers to a rival. Quality levels directly affect the purchasing patterns of customers. High standards of quality need to be maintained by businesses. Through the suppliers for raw materials to the finished products, quality must be of fundamental and paramount importance. As a business grows it will have more power to demand higher standards of quality from suppliers, making it easier to achieve a high quality product yourself.

There are Trading Standards Departments, various quality institutes (such as the British Standards Institute) and government bodies which ensure that businesses are serious about the quality of the products and services which they offer to the consumer market. Furthermore, ombudsmen services are employed to resolve disputes between consumers and specific industries which they independently police.

## Quality Control and Quality Assurance

Quality control is an important element of achieving a quality product or service. It ensures that a minimum level of quality (hopefully a quite high minimum standard) needs to be maintained and established by the business. There are several advantages for the business, including:

- Building up a strong brand and range of products
- Increase in profits through higher prices that ensures greater quality
- Minimising advertising costs as the brand is known for its unique quality
- Increase in the lifecycle of the product
- Strong consumer loyalty and affiliation with brand

Problems identified during a quality control process must be rectified before the product reaches the consumer.

Methods which can be used include self-inspection of the business; checking the quality standards of the business machinery and inspection of finished goods prior to the consumers receiving them.

The four stages of quality control are:

- Prevention
- Detection
- Correction
- Improvement

A business that strives to maintain excellent quality control standards is on course for repeated success.

**Systems of Quality Assurance**

Total Quality Management (TQM) is a concept that was introduced in the 1980's by W. Edwards Deming; he proposed the concept after studying Japanese manufacturing techniques. It requires every aspect of the business to be fully committed to ensuring high quality control standards from the initial design concept to after-sales and final delivery of product or service.

TQM strives to surpass the expectations of consumers. Quality circles are an integral aspect of TQM; these involve regular group meeting that discuss quality issues and the provision of feasible solutions for the business. It is measured by:

- Cost reductions
- Quality improvements
- Employee attitudes

**Benchmarking**

This process compares a business with its competitors and examines how its quality standards are measured in comparison to the best practices of its competitors. It is used to:

- Set business standards
- Analyse business performance in comparison with competitors
- Provide new ideas and solutions to quality issues

Kaizen is a Japanese term which means continuous improvement. Hence when applied in business, every aspect of the business appreciates the importance of taking advantage of all opportunities for enhancement and development, which will ultimately lead to delivery of the best possible products and services to the business.

# Quality Standards

There are several quality standard techniques which businesses employ. These include:

- British Standards - The British Standards Institute is the pre-eminent standards body in the world, and the national standards body of the United Kingdom. It operates across a broad spectrum from governments to manufacturing and from services to consumers. There are 27,000 standards which cover every type of product or service. The most internationally recognisable standard is the ISO 9001 Quality Management Systems Requirements. Over 670,000 organisations use this standard across 154 countries

- Poka-Yoka - Poka-Yoka was a concept developed by Shigeo Shingo. It focuses on proofing a specific process or product against any possibility of mistakes. Hence it strives to eliminate errors and if there are errors, the products should be designed in such a manner as to instantly detect and correct.

- Training - Training of the employees over a period of time is a vital way of ensuring they understand and appreciate the work role and responsibilities which it entails. Therefore, well trained staff will equate to better quality products.

- The five Ss - The five Ss are central to production and quality. It is based on the Andon system which enables workers to set-up sign boards which should be used once an error in production has been made and can be detected. This is one of the principal elements of Jidoka system or autonomation. These five Ss are:
    - Seiri – (Sort) focuses on proper arrangement of work
    - Seiton – (Shine) focuses on orderliness
    - Seiso – (Set in Order) focuses on cleanliness
    - Seiketsu – (Standardise) focuses on after-use cleanliness
    - Shitsuke – (Sustain) focuses on discipline

**Self-assessment questions**

1) In what ways can effective operations development affect the quality of the business?

2) Distinguish between Quality Control and Quality Assurance.

3) Explain the systems of Quality Assurance.

4) Highlight the issues of quality standards which affect the business.

**Student Activity 40**

Log onto the internet and read the following article:

http://www.theguardian.com/sustainable-business/sustainability-with-john-elkington/sustainability-new-total-quality-management

**How to Meet Customer Expectations**

Any business must take care of its customers, the end-users of the products and services it creates.

The satisfaction of the consumer is paramount to any business. The higher the satisfaction that a consumer derives from a product or service, the more of that product or service they are likely to use in the future.

This trend leads to brand loyalty and the high recommendation of the products of the business.

Training of employees, the use of market research, quality assurance, control and standards are used to achieve the high expectations of customers.

Qualitative market research is used to investigate customer attitudes and views, and was discussed earlier in this course.

**Activity 41 – Think of some products or services you use repeatedly because they meet or exceed your expectations.**

**Ways of monitoring and improving Customer Service**

Businesses can only achieve customer satisfaction if they can measure satisfaction successfully. Ultimate customer satisfaction can only be achieved through a process of monitoring the levels of satisfaction and benefits which the customer receives from the usage of a product or service. It involves:

- Informal feedback from customer
- The use of customer questionnaires
- Employee feedback on observation, complaints and concerns of customers
- Mystery shopping
- Complaint and compliment evaluation from customers

Evaluation and improving customer service can be achieved through an assessment of the following:

- Levels of compliments and complaints
- Levels of sales
- Staff turnover
- New customers
- Customer recommendations
- Repeat customers who are satisfied with products

**Activity 42 – Why do you think a high staff turnover can lead to lower customer satisfaction?**

**Achieving high levels of customer service and its benefits**

Businesses that understand the importance of customer satisfaction will act to take every measure that they can to meet and exceed customer expectations.

Maintaining high levels of customer satisfaction has a wide range of benefits for the business, including:

- An increase in the reputation and goodwill of the business
- Consumer confidence in the business
- Increase in the profitability of the business
- Increase in the level of sales
- Reduction in costs of advertising
- Happy and content consumers

In addition to the above, the business must take adequate precautionary measures that will prevent any unwarranted situations and accidents or anything that could pose a risk to the customer.

Health and safety is often said to be the most import priority of a business, and it always needs to be embraced as a concept.

In many industries, contracts can be won and lost because of a company's health & safety record.

**Self-assessment questions**

1) Highlight the methods of effective operations development in customer service.
2) Give reasons for the importance of a business meeting customer expectations.
3) Explain the methods of monitoring and improving customer service.
4) Discuss the benefits of achieving high levels of customer service.

## Topic 2.5 - External Influences

**Learning Outcome**

The aim of this section is for students to understand the following:

- Economic Influences
- Legislation
- The Competitive Environment

**Economic Influences**

Every business is influenced by the economic environment in one way or another. These economic factors are sometimes internal and sometimes external and outside of the businesses control.

There are a number of factors which are influential in determining the levels of business activity. These include:

- Inflation rate
- Economic growth
- Exchange rates
- Gross domestic product (GDP)
- Interest rates
- Unemployment
- Government spending and taxation
- The business cycle

Markets are also affected by global issues and world markets. Hence there is the need to be opportunistic and to have a broad outlook. Through globalisation, the business can:

- Expand into multinational economies
- Increase international trade
- Experience free movement of its workers between several countries

Strategies which the business can utilise to take advantage of globalisation include the following:

- Export of products to wider markets
- Off-shoring and having overseas locations
- Business expansion through international takeovers and merger opportunities
- Pan-global or pan-European international marketing strategies which are used by businesses to market products and service to accommodate for the local culture of the business

**Developments in emerging markets**

Emerging markets are markets which have characteristically low to middle income GDP per head. Countries that have been identified as emerging economies include the so called BRIC countries:

B - Brazil

R - Russia

I - India

C - China

Businesses need to develop the most effective strategies in order to enter emerging market. At the same time, due consideration must be given to the socio-political and economic climate of the country.

Relationship between business and the political and legal environment

There are implications of the political and legal environment for a business aimed at achieving success in its market. It is important to understand that the government is prone to intervening in the conditions of the market for several reasons.

Government economic policies include:

- Maintaining a low rate of inflation
- Wealth and income distribution
- Maintaining a low rate of unemployment
- Ensuring balance of payment equilibrium
- Sustained growth of the economy
- Environmental protection

In order to achieve these objectives the government uses:

- Monetary policy – This is used by the Bank of England to set the interest rates. It tends to have several implications for the business in export trade as it affects exchange rates
- Supply-side policy – This is used by the government in its drive to enhance the efficient performance of the economy. It includes reduction in rates of direct taxation and the expansion of courses at universities to increase the specialist skill set in the proportion of the working population
- Fiscal policy – This is used by the government to regulate the economy through the use of its taxation policies on corporation tax, income tax, excise duty and estates tax. This can impact on consumer spending as individuals have more or less disposable income for non-essential items

Political decisions which affect the business can include the move towards expansion of free trade and the ever growing influence of the European Union.

Through the World Trade Organisation there has been an increase in pressure for the enhancement of free trade among its members and the reduction of protectionism; this has had varying degrees of success.

There is a great deal of legislation which affects the way businesses conducts their activities. These include laws on Health and Safety, consumer protection and employment and anti-discrimination.

In planning for the acquisition or development of industrial, commercial or residential properties in rural and urban areas, it is mandatory that relevant planning permission must be in sought. This is based on the Town and Country Planning Acts 1947 and 1990.

In order to protect the environment, the Environmental Protection Act 1990 was passed by the Government. This restricts the emissions and pollutions which are by-products of business processes and activities.

Competition policy is also used regulate competitive behaviour of businesses within industries.

## Relationship between business and the social environment

Among the many factors which affect businesses are the ethical and social environment in which it operates; these are influenced by the attitudes and demographic make-up of society.

Demographic factors which affect the social environment include:

- Gender issues
- Ethnic groups
- Religion
- Community conditions
- Education

Demographic factors include facts about the population based on past information and predicted trends in the future. Knowledge of such information is beneficial to the business in achieving its aims of profitability and client satisfaction.

Environmental issues also affect the business, and this trend is only set to rise. These issues include carbon footprints, global warming, reduction of the quality of urban air and the use of non-sustainable resources. Most businesses now have Corporate Social Responsibility Reports (CSR) that enables them to be aware of the effects of the business activities on the environment.

With the increase in moral and ethical awareness of such issues, businesses have become more responsible in implementing ethical procedures and striving to safeguard the interests of animal welfare and fairness in labour conditions of its imported products and advertising.

**Relationship between Business and the Technological Environment**

Through the development of information technology, many businesses have been able to grow and develop beyond what would otherwise have been possible. The benefits of technological change on the business include:

- Creation of new opportunities for marketing
- Cost savings in operations management
- Development of new products
- Enabling avenues for new market opportunities to be developed

The more the business is able to exploit technological change effectively, the more it is likely to benefit from this change.

Several limitations to the use of technological change and its advancements include:

- Potential for increase in redundancies and human resources-related issues
- Speed of change in technology leads to ease of obsolescence of current IT systems. Hence there must be constant changes which involve costs and time
- Resistance to change by the existing management culture

There are a number of qualitative factors which must be taken into account when making strategic choices. These include potential customer gains, workers' and management attitude to change in technology which may be difficult to comprehend.

**Self-assessment questions**

1) Highlight the importance of assessing changes in the Business Environment
2) What is the significance of the relationship between business and the economic environment?
3) Discuss how the social and technological environment have a strong relationship on the business

## The Competitive Environment

## Relationship between Business and the Competitive Environment

The nature of the industry and environment in which the business competes will always play a major role on the activities of the business.

This is important because the competitive environment affects the profitability of the business within its specific industry. It also affects the number of available choices open to consumers. Consumer choice is sometimes restricted by businesses that collude and engage in agreements that are anti-competitive and not in the interests of consumers.

The purchasing power of consumers is affected as the nature of competition within the business environment changes.

Governmental competition policy is a tool that is used to regulate anti-competitive business practices. These anti-competitive practices are usually seen as illegal and hence legislation is usually put in place to combat such malpractices within the industry.

The Office of Fair Trading (OFT) executed the policies of competition enacted by the European Union and the United Kingdom. This was done through the release of reports to the media about collusive practices between firms thereby creating bad publicity for such firms.

Furthermore, it imposed fines on firms for exhibiting anti-competitive behaviour. It also refused permission on proposals of acquisitions and mergers, which would ultimately create a dominant firm in an industry that could be monopolistic and against the best interest of the public.

The Office of Fair Trading was responsible for protecting consumer interests throughout the UK. It closed on 01 April 2014, with its responsibilities passing to a number of different organisations including the Competition and Markets Authority (CMA) and the Financial Conduct Authority.

**Legislation**

Changes in legislation impact hugely on businesses and can affect their business practices in addition to impacting on their activities. Legislation covers:

- Consumer protection
- Employee protection
- Environmental protection
- Competition policy
- Health and safety

Consumer protection includes the Sale of Goods act 1979 – where goods must be described as of satisfactory quality and fit for purpose. Once a consumer purchases a product they enter into a legally binding contract with the seller and are afforded protection under this law, if something doesn't met that requirement.

Employees are covered by a number of different legislation in regard to protecting their employment status and also the opportunities that they are offered with work. Legislation includes: National minimum wage act 1998, where employees are to receive a minimum wage per hour based on their age. This was introduced to give individuals a living wage and to reduce individual's reliance on welfare payments. Other laws are in place to protect individuals from discrimination and being offered less opportunities as their colleagues such as Disability Discrimination Act 1995.

Environmental protection looks at businesses reducing the amount of packaging that they secure their products in, their wastage and their logistic methods in order to reduce their carbon footprint.

**Competition policy which has been discussed in this section previously**

Health and safety legislation is covered by the Health and safety Act 1974. This is known as an umbrella act, covering all aspects of health and safety. As technology and working practices have evolved and changed, new laws have been introduced in order to accommodate them and protect individuals and businesses alike.

These external influences are beyond the control of the business, however, businesses must adapt and change and accommodate them in order to remain competitive and profitable.

**The Competitive Environment**

**Possible impacts of market conditions and degree of competition**

The environment in which a company competes is of paramount importance to the activities of the business. For a business to analyse the industry and its competitive environment, seven issues must be considered:

- Nature and strength of competition
- Identification of any key factors which determine competitive success
- Attractiveness of the industry
- Nature of dominant features of the industry
- Impact of factors of change on the competitiveness of the industry
- Anticipation of strategic initiatives of competitors
- Knowledge and identification of key competitors

New competitors also have an impact on the market and level of competition. New entrants with strong financial resources and synergy potentials should be seen as threats, and they increase the competitiveness of the market. Buyers are seen as major influences because they can have a strong position when they possess numerous sources available for buying of products. Rivalry from direct competitors leads business to strive for extraordinary performance to out-do competition.

The business ensures that it analyses, critically evaluates and knows the move of every competitor, and how to beat such competitive rivalry. Market condition and degree competitiveness are also affected by the suppliers and the level of strength possessed by the supplier. Strong suppliers dictate the course of the market competition through the availability or scarcity of unique and difficult products. Furthermore, few suppliers also affect the market with strong demand for their products.

**Determinants of Competitiveness**

The level of competitiveness is determined by the organisation of transactions, technology, corporate strategies and characteristics of the market. Competitive advantage creates a commercial advantage of a particular business over its rivals. Porter's four generic competitive strategies describe the concept of competitive advantage.

Porter suggested that competition on price (cost leadership) or differentiation on the one hand, or whether to target a broad or narrow market are the two decisions to make in order to establish a competitive advantage. These strategies are:

- Differentiation
- Overall price or cost leadership
- Price or cost focus
- Differentiation focus

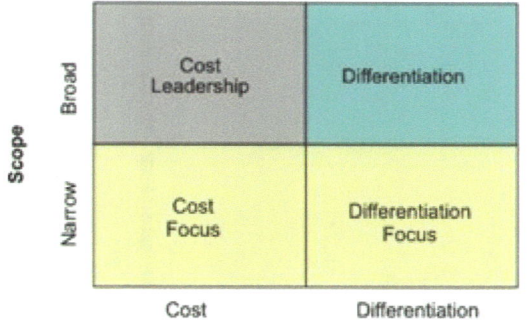

Market share also determines competitiveness in the market. This is the ratio of the business sales to the total market sales.

**Methods of Improving Competitiveness**

Competitiveness is an important objective for any business. This is because there is constant change taking place, and to attract the best customers, the business must continually re-invent itself. Methods of improving competitiveness include:

- Performance Importance grid
- SWOT Analysis
- Competitive Strategies
- Macro Environment
- Competitive Intelligence

Performance importance grid

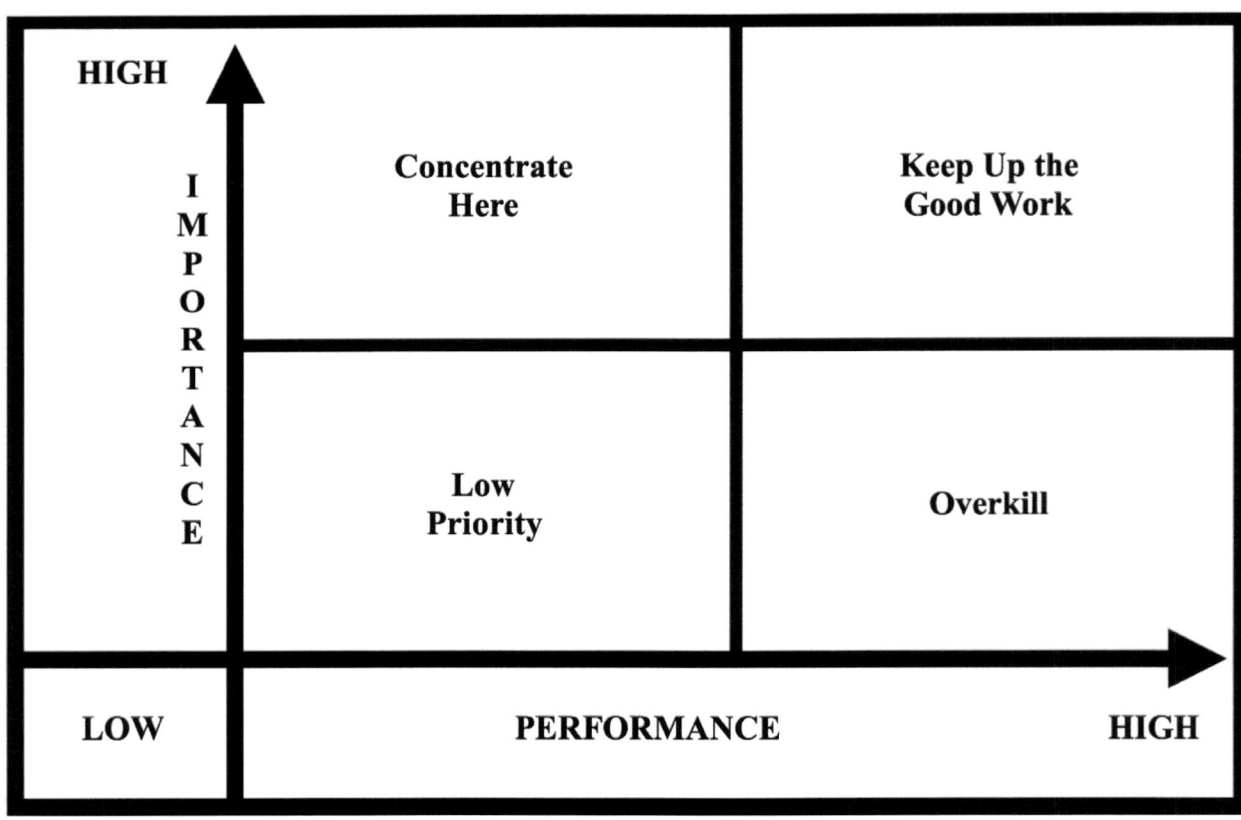

The above grid is used to identify current strengths, weaknesses and priorities of a business in specific areas of the business. Through the identification of current successes and priorities in the business operations can formulate the right strategies which relate to these two criteria.

**SWOT analysis**

This is used to examine the business from an overall perspective. It identifies the strengths, weaknesses, threats and opportunities that the business faces.

## Competitive strategies

These are a combination of strategies of a business and are aimed at maintaining the competitive edge of the business.

Macro environmental factors are caused by the effect of the external activities that may have an impact on the business activities. Once these external issues have been identified, the business can act accordingly to ensure that the business activities are optimally used.

Competitive Intelligence (CI) is used to provide input into a whole range of decision-making processes. It involves collection of information, conversion of collated data information to intelligence, communication of the intelligence information obtained and acting on the information, including its use to counter adverse competitor action.

**Activity 43 – What do you think are the drawbacks of the SWOT analysis approach?**

**Self-assessment questions**

1) Discuss the relationship between marketing and competitiveness
2) What are the possible impacts of market conditions and degree of competition for a business?
3) Describe the determinants of competitiveness
4) Explain the methods which can be used by a business to improve competitiveness

# Theme 3

# Business Decision and Strategy

Topic 3.1 - Business Objectives and Strategy

Topic 3.2 - Business Growth

Topic 3.3 - Decision-Making Techniques

Topic 3.4 - Influences on Business Decisions

Topic 3.5 - Assessing Competitiveness

Topic 3.6 - Managing Change

**Topic 3.1 - Business Objectives and Strategy**

**Learning Outcome**

The aim of this section is for students to understand the following:

- Corporate Objectives
- Theories of Corporate Strategy
- SWOT Analysis
- Impact of External Influences

**Corporate Objectives**

Corporate aims can be defined as the goals of the business over the long-term period. They are used as a means to determine the direction and focus of the business. The mission statement of the business is used to communicate the corporate aims to all the stakeholders of the business. The corporate objectives are statements which quantify the goals of a business in order for it to achieve its long-term aims. They are influenced by the age of the business, its culture and the nature of the sector. Corporate strategies are medium to long-term plans of the business which detail how the company intends to achieve its corporate objectives. These strategies could be:

- Generic strategies
- Operational strategies
- Global strategies
- Corporate strategies

In order for a company to achieve its strategic development targets, it can combine several ideas and aims, such as internal development, synergy and external growth.

Corporate objectives are created at the top of management as illustrated below:

**Stakeholder influences**

Stakeholders of a business come from a range of backgrounds but they are all very important, and each has a major impact on the activities of the business.

Stakeholders all have a different perspective on the business, and have their own aspirations for it. For example:

- Employees seek pay rises and improved working conditions
- Managers might expect bonus payments
- Creditors expect healthy cash flow
- Investors expect a return
- The Inland Revenue expect tax to be paid in full and on time
- The government wants the business to be legally compliant
- Customers expect good quality products and services, and a consistency of supply

There are times when potential conflicts of interest arise between the business and various stakeholder groups. However, the business is not under any obligation to take into consideration the perspectives of any stakeholder group.

**Activity 44 – Think of a business you are familiar with and list the stakeholders.**

Corporate objectives need to be clearly defined once the mission of the company and its aims are known. Such goals always need to be measurable in order that an assessment can be made as to the progress of the business.

Functional objectives facilitate the fulfilment of corporate objectives; hence, through coordination between departments, this becomes achievable.

Small to medium-sized companies make it easier to achieve these goals. However, in larger business and corporations these are more difficult to achieve.

**Activity 45 – Give an example of a strategic level objective.**

There is a relationship between functional and corporate objectives as shown below:

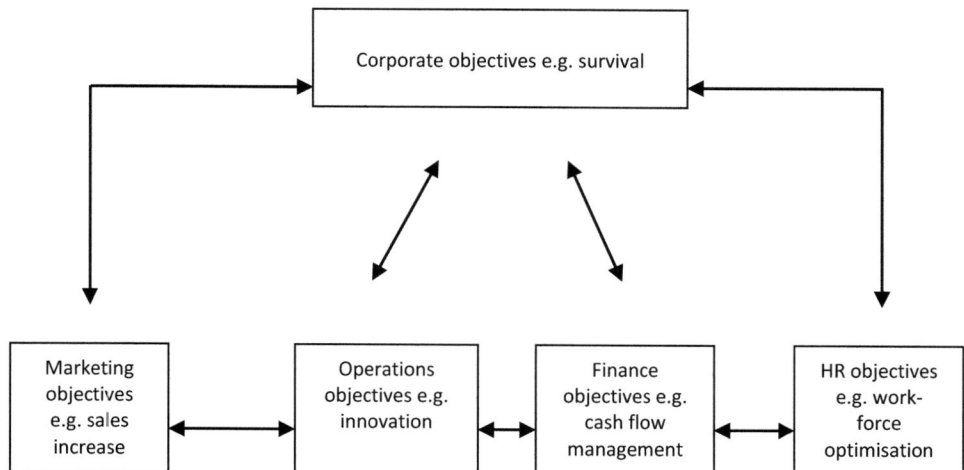

## Functional Strategies

These strategies develop from the functional objectives of the business. They need to be measurable and specific. Through team consultation these plans are implemented in order to ensure feasibility. Functional objectives need to be SMART targets:

S - Specific
M - Measurable
A - Agreed
R - Realistic
T - Time-based

The relationship between functional strategies and objectives is shown below:

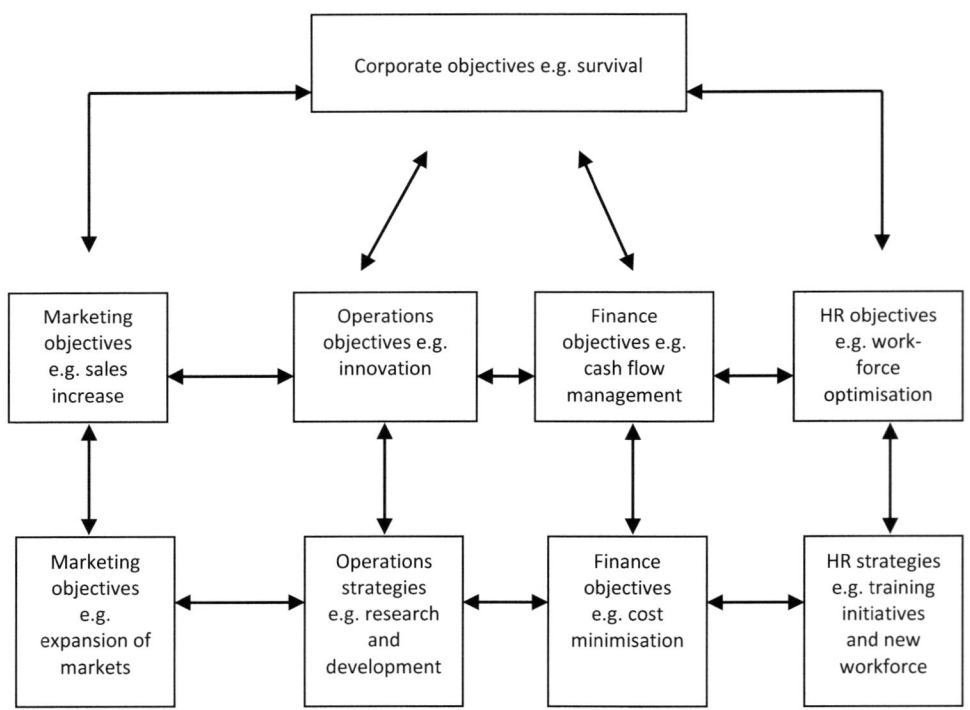

**Self-assessment questions**

1) Discuss the functional objectives and strategies of a business
2) How can a business utilise its objectives and strategies to achieve optimum result?
3) Discuss the merits and limitations of functional objectives and strategies of a business

**Activity 46 -**

Log onto the internet and look at the following organisations' mission statements.

http://www.starbucks.co.uk/about-us/company-information/mission-statement

http://www.virginactive.co.uk/about-us/who-we-are

http://www.levistrauss.com/who-we-are

**Theories of Corporate Strategy**

Corporate strategy is concerned with management making high-level decisions to decide where the business wants to be and how it is going to get there. Decisions are made about the following:

- Running the business – organising resources effectively and efficiently
- Meeting the needs and expectations of customers
- Creating a competitive advantage
- Achieving Corporate Objectives

There are several models which can assist an organisation in developing corporate strategies.

Ansoff's Matrix

This matrix is a marketing planning tool that determines product and market growth strategy. This matrix examines new and existing products of the business, and whether the market is new or existing. With the explicit aim of creating a list of growth strategies which will determine the direction of the business strategy.

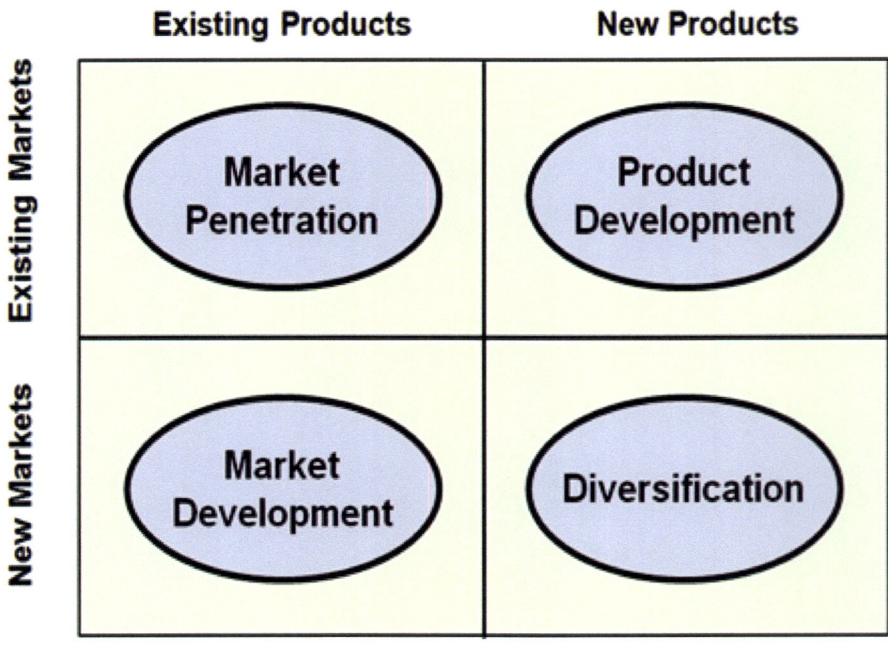

The key features of Ansoff's Matrix are:

- Market Penetration – selling products into existing market and creating a growth strategy. Adapting the marketing mix in order to exploit product sales
- Market Development – selling of existing products into new markets, which can be a higher risk as the business, enters new markets
- Product Development – this is where the business aims to launch new products into existing markets. This may mean a strategy of new competencies and the development of modified products that appeal to existing markets
- Diversification – this is a growth strategy of new products in new markets. This is very high-risk strategy for the business as they enter unknown markets

Porter's Strategic Matrix

This is a matrix to assist businesses to achieve a sustainable competitive advantage over competitors. This competitive advantage may be by offering lower prices for the product or service or offering the customer greater value.

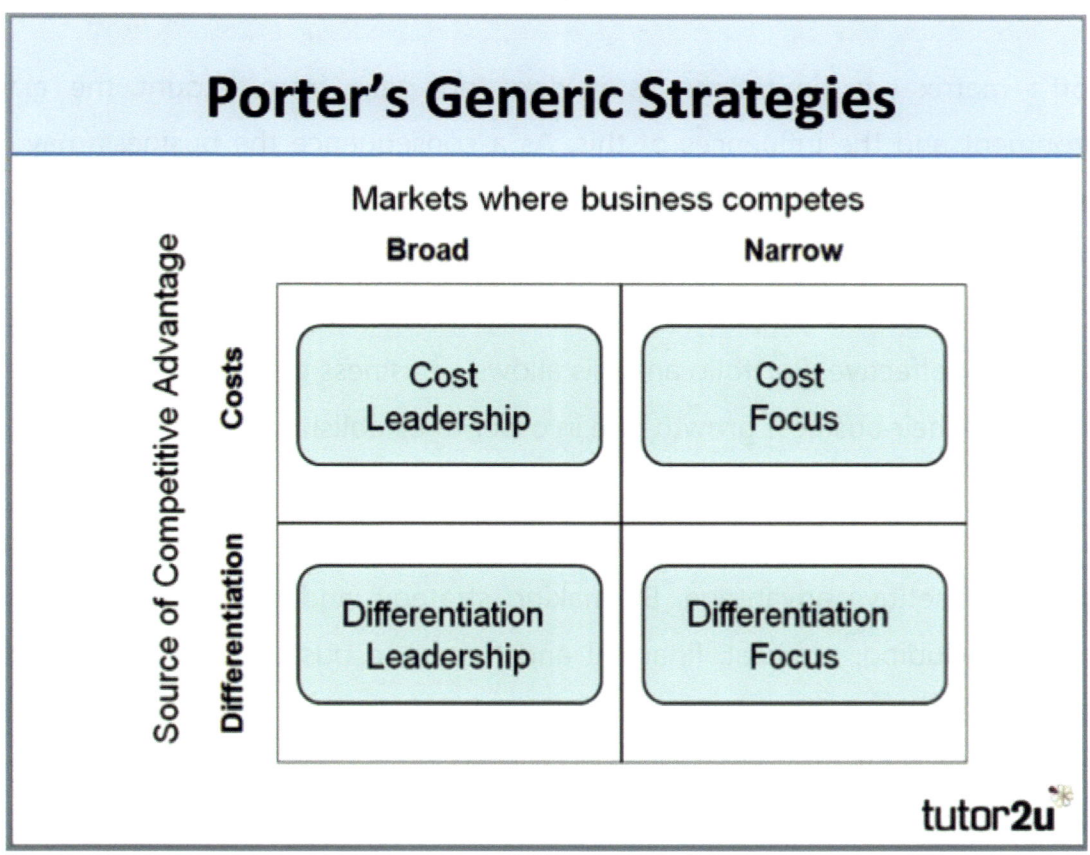

The key features of Porter's matrix are:

- Cost leadership – this strategy is the low cost producer and the business will need to exploit economies of scales to minimise the cost of production
- Cost focus – this is where the business reduces the cost of the product in just one or two market segments. The product is likely to be basic, perhaps similar to a high priced market leader
- Differentiation Focus – this strategy aims to differentiate with a small number of target market segments. This is a 'niche' marketing strategy where customers have specific needs for the product or service. The business needs to differentiate themselves from competitors by delivering high quality customers needs and wants
- Differentiation Leadership – this is where the business targets large markets to achieve competitive advantage across the whole industry. The product is usually associated with a premium price and extra value added features for the customer. Strong brands like Nike or Audi use this strategy

Ansoff's matrix has limitations as it does not take into account the external environment and the influences of this. As a consequence the business may make strategic decisions that fail. The matrix also does not look at the required resources such as distribution channels that the business will need. Porter's matrix has limitations in that it does not take into account the costs of differentiation to the business and if it will be cost effective. Portfolio analysis allows a business to assess their competitive position and their business growth rate in order to establish sound strategic planning.

By exceeding the profits considered average within a market, a business is considered to have competitive advantage. By making strategic and tactical decisions on all resources including: physical, financial and human, a business can maintain those capabilities and succeed, where others have failed to. This is known as distinctive capabilities, where the business fully utilises all of its resources to gain advantage over its competitors.

The decisions made by the business can have an impact on its resources creating a higher demand of them. Whether the business needs to invest more finance in order to achieve its strategies or employ more specialised staff. To make full use of these matrices they need to be considered in conjunction with a SWOT and PESTLE analysis.

SWOT Analysis

Businesses must know what threats and opportunities there are both within the business and externally in order to plan and make decisions effectively. This whole assessment of the strengths, weakness, opportunities and threats is known as a SWOT analysis.

- The benefits of small businesses include:
- Identification of potential new market opportunities
- Identification of strengths upon which to build
- Identification of weaknesses which can be improved upon
- Identification of threats to the existing business, perhaps from competitors

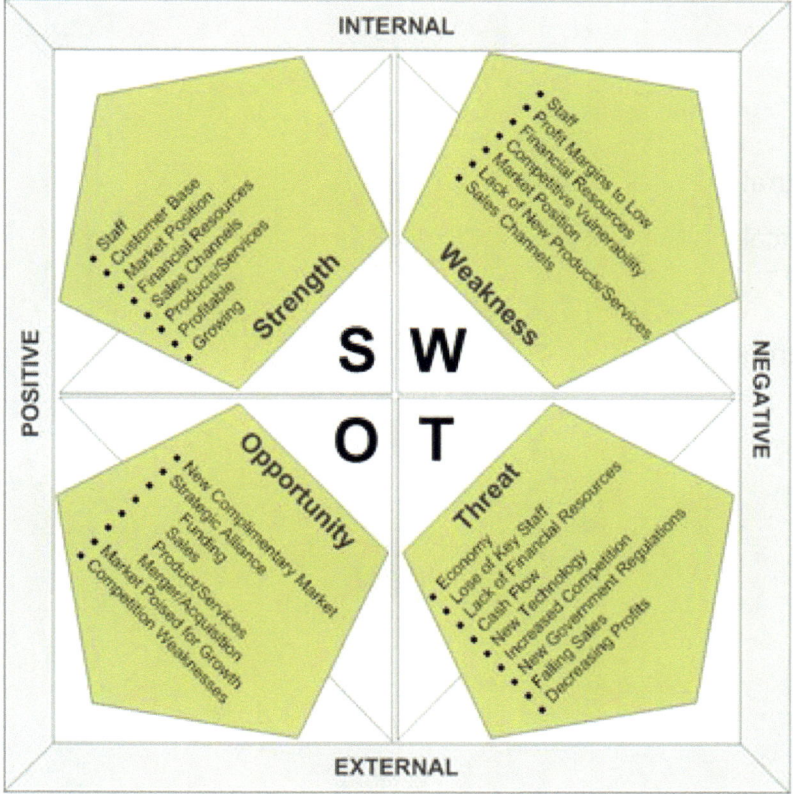

A SWOT analysis is a strategic tool which helps a business to analyse its resources and the environment. A SWOT analysis looks at internal strengths, internal weaknesses, opportunities in the external environment and threats in the external environment.

The purpose of a SWOT analysis is to:

- Investigate what the business does better than the competition
- Investigate what the competition does better
- Ask how the business is making the most of the opportunities available
- Ask how the business will respond to changes in the external environment
- The results of this analysis will identify positive and negative factors that management need to act on to improve the business

PESTLE Analysis

PESTLE is used as an external analysis of the environment, and identifies factors that the business needs to takes into consideration.

P = Political
E = Economic
S = Socio-cultural
T = Technological
L = Legal
E = Environmental

Political factors – governments influence business through tax policies or trade agreements. Which political party is in government at the time will have an influence on business. This can be favourable through low taxation or agreeable trading, or negatively impact on the business with high taxation and trade restrictions.

Economic factors – looks at the wider economy such as local and national employment figures, economic growth, costs of raw materials, interest rates, exchange rates, inflation and monetary policies. All these will influence the business.

Socio-Cultural Factors – this looks at the culture of the society the business operates in. This will include age distribution, population growth, demographics, wealth distribution, and skill levels of the population, social class and living standards.

Technological Factors – this looks at new developments and inventions. This can be the internet and web developments, but it can also be new methods of production in manufacturing.

Legal Factors – these can be new national employment laws or international trade restrictions or regulations.

Environmental Factors – this looks at natural resources, recycling and waste disposal. Organisations need to be mindful of fines and damage to their reputation if they pollute the environment.

Porter's Five Forces

This model is a framework for analysing the nature of competition in an industry. Porter identified five forces that act together to determine the nature of competition:

These forces are:

- Threat of market entry – when a new business moves into the industry, they will gain a market share and will rival existing business. For new entrants there will be barriers to entering the market; the stronger these barriers are means existing organisations will be better placed. If the barriers to entry are low, the threat of the new entrants will be high. For example, high investment set up costs, regulatory and legal restrictions, product differentiation and branding and access to suppliers

- Power of Suppliers – if suppliers have bargaining power they will sell their products at the highest price and this will affect the business profits. Suppliers are in a powerful position when there are few large suppliers, if resources of supply are scarce, if the service to the customer is high and loyal customers are reluctant to go elsewhere. The cost of switching to a new supplier for the business is high

- Power of Customer – if the customer has bargaining power they can drive down prices of the product or increase the quality of the product for the same price. Customers have bargaining power if they are placing large orders to the supplier (economies of scale) or there are a number of suppliers where the customer can 'shop around' for the best deal. Supermarkets are a good example of this for groceries and milk products

- Threat from Substitutes – this is a product that meets the same customer need but is produced from a different industry. Substitutes are a threat as they will limit the price charged and reduce an organisation's profits. The threat is dependent on customer loyalty not to switch products, and the quality of the substitute product

**The Changing Competitive Environment**

Competition in an industry encourages businesses to make competitive price reductions, invest in innovation and new products and advertise their products by spending money on marketing.

The competitive environment is affected by the following:

- Number of competitors in the market
- Market size and growth opportunities
- Product differentiation and brand loyalty
- Power of buyers and available substitutes

**Activity 47 -**

Log onto the internet and watch an interview with Michael Porter about the Five Forces model.
https://www.youtube.com/watch?v=mYF2_FBCvXw

**Topic 3.2 - Business Growth**

**Learning Outcome**

The aim of this section is for students to understand the following:

- Growth
- Mergers and Takeovers
- Organic Growth
- Reasons for Staying Small

**Growth**

The growth of the firm is achieved as the firm generates enough profits and sales from the sale of the output it produces. The growth of the firm in a market is the percentage increment in its size in relation to its share of the market. As a firm secures a greater market size this should also correspond to the total sales by the firm as it supplies products or services within the market.

There are various types of growth of the firm:

- Internal growth
- External growth
- Mergers and Acquisitions
- Integration

These will be discussed later in this section.

**Economies of scale**

Economies of scale occur when a firm experiences a reduction in the costs of production of outputs, as it expands and makes more output. Hence, as output rises, the cost of producing the output decreases. The decrease in costs is experienced over a period of time, and it does not happen instantly. Firms can benefit from the economies of scale only after a period of time, during which the other factor inputs have experienced changes. An assumption is that the prices of all the other factor inputs remain the same.

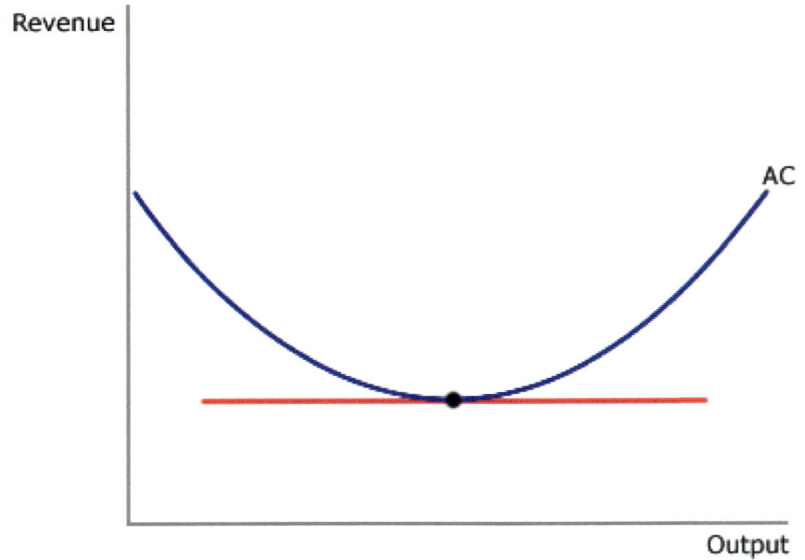

A firm can experience internal and external economies of scale that would enable it to see tremendous growth in output and a corresponding dramatic reduction of its costs. Internal economies of large-scale production result, due to the growth of the business of the firm. They include:

- Financial economies
- Technological economies
- Marketing economies
- Managerial economies

External economies of large-scale production happen due to the growth in the size of the industry as the average costs of the various firms in the industry fall over a period of time.

The factors that can make external economies of scale include:

- The sharing of research and development costs by the various firms which reduces the burden more than if a firm were to solely bear the responsibility
- The existence of joint suppliers who specialise in manufacturing the components for the whole industry, which works out to be cheaper for all the firms than if each firm had to manufacture their own components
- Establishment of institutions which provide training for the members of staff across the industry, thereby reducing the costs of each firm providing their respective training needs

**Diseconomies of scale**

Diseconomies of scale occur when a firm grows beyond the point where its costs over a long period of time increase despite its increasing output. This occurs when a firm producing a specific item is running at full capacity.

In order to produce a larger output, the firm would have to invest in new capital goods e.g. a new factory or machinery etc. These diseconomies of scale could be internal or external.

Internal diseconomies of scale include:

- Problems which relate to monitoring individual performance of staff in a large organisation. This leads to a serious problem of control
- An increase in staff also means that there can be a reduction in productivity because of lack of motivation of members of staff who do not see their roles as pivotal to the business
- The co-ordination of complex processes in the production of goods and services can be a huge task. An example of this is trying to ensure that the flow of information is efficient
- The requirement to purchase or build a new factory to produce another unit

External diseconomies of scale include:

- Rise in cost of raw materials for the inputs. This can happen due to an increase in demand because of the growth of the industry
- Increase in the cost of transportation. Where there are geographical economies of scale and the large concentration of numerous firms, there tends to be congestion, and this will increase the costs of transportation of raw materials and finished products over time

**Mergers and Takeovers**

External growth of the firm occurs through mergers, acquisitions and takeovers. These are aggressive means of expansion which the firm and large corporations use to enlarge their market share. A merger is a combination of two separate businesses into a new business. A takeover is where one business acquires a controlling interest into another business. A business that mergers with another or is involved in a takeover needs to consider the strategic and tactical benefits to the organisation.

Strategic Choice:

- Access new markets
- Improved distribution networks
- Improved brand awareness
- Tactical Choice:
- Increase market share
- Access new technology
- Increase skill and competency of employees

Integration is where organisations integrate with one another. There are different types.

Forward vertical integration is where one organisation merges with another at the next stage of production. For example, a coffee bean producer purchases coffee shops.

Backwards vertical integration is where an organisation integrates with another in a stage of production further away from the customer. For example, a car manufacturer buys a tyre manufacturer.

Horizontal integration is where there two organisations at the same stage of production join together.

Advantages and disadvantages of integrations are:

- Vertical integration – the advantages are greater control over supply chain, reduction in costs, improvement in quality. The disadvantages are different cultures, diseconomies of scale and less choice for the customer
- Horizontal integration – the advantages are economies of scale, spread risk and reduce the competition. Disadvantages are different cultures and diseconomies of scale
- Conglomerate integration – advantages are a reduced risk by operating in a different market, increased knowledge of another market. Disadvantages are that there will be an organisational culture difference and employees with different skills

Disadvantages for merger and takeover are as follows:

- High Costs
- Clash of different organisational cultures
- Customers may be unhappy or upset
- Incompatibility of management styles
- Resistance from employees who may be concerned about their employment
- Organic Growth

Internal growth of the firm is also known as organic growth. It involves a strong reliance on capital to expand and internal resources, which it uses to enhance its growth and enrich the firm structure. Successful organic growth internally involves a through re-assessment of the business practices to determine areas of improvements. This is followed by a workable plan of action to expand from within, which leads to implementing an action plan that works.

Organic growth can be achieved through new product launches, expanding opening new stores, expanding into foreign markets and expansion of the workforce.

Advantages of organic growth are:

- It is less expensive
- There is a reduced risk as the business has more control of the variables
- Existing management culture will remain
- Growth can be controlled
- Disadvantages of organic growth are:
- Growth can be slow and limited
- Staff skills and competency may be limited
- Financial limitations

**Reasons for Staying Small**

A small business can offer a personal service to the customer by offering product differentiation. A small business can offer USP (unique selling point) by having 'bespoke' or exclusive products. A small business can respond to customer needs quickly with a personalised service and develop a good relationship, which attracts brand loyalty. To survive in a competitive world, small businesses need to develop e-commerce and trade their products on-line.

**Topic 3.3 - Decision-Making Techniques**

**Learning Outcome**

The aim of this section is for students to understand the following:

- Quantitative Sales Forecasting
- Investment Appraisal
- Decision Trees
- Critical Path Analysis

# Quantitative Sales Forecasting and Investment Appraisal

Investment decisions are frequently made in relation to capital expenditure. Making the right investment decisions is critical in improving the profitability and overall growth potential of a business. Scientific decision-making tools can be used to analyse whether or not a particular capital investment project is worthwhile. Net present value, payback and average rate of return are the three commonly used techniques.

Quantitative sales forecasting uses numerical facts and prior experience to predict the sales that a business will yield. This relies on extrapolation, which is predicting future trends on what has happened in the past, making the assumption that little changes.

A forecast can predicted through a mathematical calculation or by drawing a graph such as a scatter graph, where the predicted sales are plotted against months of the year. As long as the graph shows an overall positive trend the business will be successful. However, this can be an unreliable tool as predictability and stability are rare. This prediction over time called time-series analysis, varies due to seasonal influences or factors that cannot be predicted.

While more umbrellas maybe sold in November, there is little point in comparing those sales with the sales the previous year in July. The key is to identify the trend over a period of time and see what the trend of sales is. Ignoring seasonal or cyclical factors.

Moving averages take into consideration seasonal trends and for variations in sales of each quarter of the year. This allows the business to take an average of sales of each quarter. This has limitations as the average will also be less than the raw data. This method is appropriate when the external business environment is stable, such as the competition when it is not expected to change. It will not benefit a business though when there are periods of instability or change.

## Payback period

This is a basic but effective method of determining the financial viability of a project. The payback period is defined as being the time it will take to get a financial return on the initial investment.

Consider a situation where a company wished to invest in a piece of equipment that is required for a project with a five-year life cycle. There are two competing machines that will perform the same function; each costs the same and is no more difficult than the other to install or operate. How does a project manager choose between them?

Each machine will generate cash flow at a different rate throughout the project as follows:

| Year | Cash Flow of Machine A | Cash Flow of Machine B |
|------|------------------------|------------------------|
| 1 | £20,000 | £5,000 |
| 2 | £20,000 | £10,000 |
| 3 | £10,000 | £10,000 |
| 4 | £10,000 | £20,000 |
| 5 | £5,000 | £20,000 |
| Total | £65,000 | £65,000 |

Each machine generates the same amount of total income. If each machine costs £40,000 pounds, what is the payback period for machine A and machine B?

Given that the payback period is the time it takes to generate profit, you can easily see that machine A's payback period is 2 years and machine B is 4 years. Most project managers, given this situation would select machine A, although there may well be many other factors that you will have to take into account. The payback period method has both advantages and disadvantages over other methods of project selection criteria.

Advantages:

- Simplicity – As you saw above, it is extremely easy to use, if you have the correct data to analyse
- The data is usually easy to determine or estimate
- Exposure to project risk is reduced if you choose the project with the shortest payback period. A longer payback period of, say, 4 years as in the example, could suffer from unexpected external factors like recession
- It is useful in highly technological environments where technology is rapidly changing

Disadvantages:

- Inflation is not considered. Money becomes less valuable over time. It is better to have £100 today than the promise of £100 in 10 years' time
- It is a short-term indicator. Projects with an expected life cycle or payback period that is 5 years or more should not be selected using this method as there are far too many external factors that can influence the project that are not considered
- The cash flows are estimates, and estimates can always be wrong
- The payback period does not consider the whole project, only part of it

Consider the following example:

| Year | Cash Flow of Machine A | Cash Flow of Machine B |
|------|------------------------|------------------------|
| 1 | £20,000 | £5,000 |
| 2 | £20,000 | £10,000 |
| 3 | £10,000 | £10,000 |
| 4 | £10,000 | £30,000 |
| 5 | £5,000 | £40,000 |
| Total | £65,000 | £95,000 |

Using the above data and considering the payback method, which machine would you invest in (assuming the machine costs £40,000 as previously)? Why would this be a poor choice?

The payback period is the same as in the first example, and therefore you would choose machine A. What the payback period model does not consider, however, is the whole life cycle. Machine B takes longer to pay back the initial investment but it is expected to generate far more money over the life cycle of the project. The moral is: be wary when only using the payback period method.

**Return on investment (ROI)**

The Return on investment (ROI) is also a popular method of selecting a project, and it has the advantage over the payback period method of considering the whole life cycle.

The ROI method first calculates the average annual profit of a project; this is a very simple calculation:

$$\text{Average annual profit} = \frac{\text{(Total profit)} - \text{(Total outlay)}}{\text{Years the project runs}}$$

$$\text{Return on Investment} = \frac{\text{Average annual profit}}{\text{Investment}} \times \frac{100}{1}$$

| Year | Cash Flow of Machine A | Cash Flow of machine B |
|-------|------------------------|------------------------|
| 1 | £20,000 | £5,000 |
| 2 | £20,000 | £10,000 |
| 3 | £10,000 | £10,000 |
| 4 | £10,000 | £20,000 |
| 5 | £5,000 | £20,000 |
| Total | £65,000 | £65,000 |

Using the data in table 4, calculate the annual profit and ROI of the project if machine A or machine B were selected (again assuming a cost of £40,000):

Your calculations should look something like this:

$$\text{Average annual profit} = \frac{65,000 - 40,000}{5}$$

$$= £5,000$$

$$\text{Return on Investment} = \frac{5000}{40000} \quad \times \quad \frac{100}{1}$$

$$= 12.5\%$$

This means that machine A will generate 12.5% of the outlay each year for the five years of the project (on average).

The answer is the same, of course, for both machine A and machine B as the both have the same initial cost and the same total return.

| Year | Cash Flow of Machine A | Cash Flow of Machine B |
|---|---|---|
| 1 | £20,000 | £5,000 |
| 2 | £20,000 | £10,000 |
| 3 | £10,000 | £10,000 |
| 4 | £10,000 | £30,000 |
| 5 | £5,000 | £40,000 |
| Total | £65,000 | £95,000 |

Now consider two machines with different total returns, and see which you would choose. Consider the following data with machine A costing £25,000 and machine B £40,000:

Your answers should be something like the following:

Machine A:

$$\text{Average annual profit} = \frac{65000 - 25000}{5}$$

$$= £8000$$

$$\text{Return on investment} = \frac{8000}{25000} \times \frac{100}{1}$$

$$= 32\%$$

Machine B:

$$\text{Average annual profit} = \frac{95000 - 40000}{5}$$

$$= £11000$$

$$\text{Return on investment} = \frac{11000}{40000} \times \frac{100}{1}$$

$$= 27.5\%$$

## Activity 48 – Which machine should you buy?

These results take a bit more analysing than the payback period method. Machine A will generate an average of £8,000 profit per year at a ROI of 32%, not bad at all. Machine B on the other hand will generate an average of £11,000 year profit, but with the lower ROI of 27.5%.

Which machine should you buy?

This is not a simple question to answer; you may not have enough capital to invest in machine B, for example, or you may have enough to purchase two of machine A. In general terms the project with the higher ROI is generally considered the best one to invest in, even though in this specific example machine B actually generates a higher average annual profit.

Like the payback period method, the ROI method is very simple to use, and although it uses calculations, they are not difficult ones. The ROI method has the added advantage that it considers the whole of the project life cycle. The method gives two results: average profit per year of the project, and a percentage return, both of which are easily understood concepts for project managers.

One of the main drawbacks of the ROI method is that it does not distinguish when profit is made in the project life cycle. If, for example, project A makes excellent initial profit and then tails off whilst project B makes a slow start and then picks up in years 4 or 5, both could generate exactly the same results in terms of average annual profit and ROI. In this instance, project A would be more desirable as the profit comes more quickly, but the ROI method does not demonstrate this.

Both of the methods considered thus far have the drawback that they do not consider the time value of money. As noted above, £100 today will not be worth £100 in 10 years' time because of the negative effects of inflation. For this reason further models had to be developed.

**Discounted cash flow (DCF)**

The DCF models are intended to take into account inflation. They recognise the real world situation that £100 today will be able to buy more than the same amount next year or the year after (except in the exceptional economic circumstance of deflation; but we won't worry about that here.)

There are two basic DCF methods:

- Net Present Value (NPV)
- Internal rate of Return (IRR)

These two techniques enable a project manager to compare two disparate projects with different cash flows and investment profiles. The major drawback of the DCF methods is that they require an accurate estimate of future interest rates.

**Net Present Value (NPV)**

In order to understand NPV properly, we have to think about the effect inflation, or indeed compound interest, has upon the value of money. If you invested £10,000 in a bank account today at an interest rate of 6% and allowed the interest to compound, you would have the following:

| Year | Total £ |
|------|---------|
| 0 | 10,000 |
| 1 | 10,600 |
| 2 | 11,236 |
| 3 | 11,910 |
| 4 | 12,625 |
| 5 | 13,382 |

From this, it also follows that if you were offered £10,600 one year from today, that money would be worth £10,000 in today's money (assuming an interest rate of 6%). This is called the net present value, i.e. what a future amount of money is worth TODAY.

In order to calculate the NPV of a future sum of money, we need to use a discount factor. There are standard tables of these available in almost any project management textbook, and also widely on the internet, but for the sake of ease table 7 below contains some to allow us to do a few calculations.

| Year | 10% | 11% | 12% | 13% | 14% | 15% | 16% | 17% | 18% |
|---|---|---|---|---|---|---|---|---|---|
| 1 | 0.9091 | 0.9009 | 0.8929 | 0.885 | 0.8772 | 0.8696 | 0.8621 | 0.8547 | 0.8475 |
| 2 | 0.8264 | 0.8116 | 0.7972 | 0.7831 | 0.7695 | 0.7561 | 0.7432 | 0.7305 | 0.7182 |
| 3 | 0.7513 | 0.7312 | 0.7118 | 0.693 | 0.675 | 0.6575 | 0.6407 | 0.6244 | 0.6086 |
| 4 | 0.683 | 0.6587 | 0.6355 | 0.6133 | 0.5921 | 0.5718 | 0.5523 | 0.5337 | 0.5158 |
| 5 | 0.6209 | 0.5935 | 0.5674 | 0.5428 | 0.5194 | 0.4972 | 0.4761 | 0.4561 | 0.4371 |

The calculation for the NPV is:

NPV = Cash Flow x Discount Factor

Complete the NPV column in the following table (assume a discount factor of 10%):

| Year | Cash Flow | Discount Factor (10%) | NPV |
|---|---|---|---|
| 0 | 50000 | 1 | |
| 1 | 10000 | 0.9091 | |
| 2 | 20000 | 0.8264 | |
| 3 | 25000 | 0.7513 | |
| 4 | 20000 | 0.683 | |

The NPV is ultimately a means of determining if a project will actually generate money in real terms, that is to say taking into account inflation and the changing value of money. If the NPV is negative then the project should not be considered as it is expected to lose money. When considering a project, obviously the project with the highest expected NPV should be considered first.

Advantages of NPV System:

- It allows the project manager to consider the time value of money
- It allows the project manager to consider how much a project will make in today's money

Disadvantages of the NPV System:

- It is limited by the accuracy of the forecast of future interest rates
- Short term projects are more accurately predicted, long term projects are difficult to predict
- It only considers financial information. For example, the future effects of economic growth or the effects of climate change cannot be considered

These tools that you have been shown over the last few pages should not be considered to the exclusion of other data when choosing a project to support or undertake. Average rate of return (ARR) is used to assess the worth of an investment by calculating the average annual profit as a percentage of initial investment. The payback method is used to calculate the length of time in which it will take to pay back the initial cost of an investment.

The net present value (NPV) calculates the total return from an investment in current terms as of today. The criteria for investment are minimum targets which are set prior to making critical investment decisions. Furthermore, there are degrees of uncertainty and risks involved in making investment decisions. A business must analyse risk factors before making an investment decision.

**Decision Trees**

A decision tree is a model to support a business decision that considers the possible consequences such as the outcomes and resource costs. Decision trees take into account when decisions can be taken and also when chance can determine the outcome. This is calculated using probability. Decision trees are more suited to situations when a sequence of events needs to be followed and when conditions are uncertain.

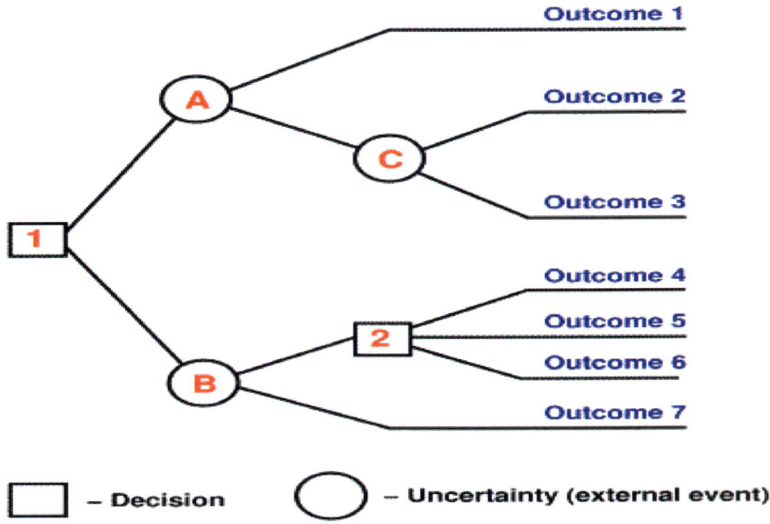

The decision tree sets out the key features of a decision, with the problem set out from left to right, and the decisions laid out in sequence. The branches show the decision to be made and also the chance events beyond the decision maker's control, taking into consideration the probability of each event.

Decision trees are a useful support tool as they are simple to understand and can be used with little explanation. They assist with the thought process to determine different scenario outcomes. Decision trees can, however, become complex where numerous variable outcomes and calculations are present.

## Critical Path Analysis

Critical path analysis is a commonly used concept in project management. It analyses a set of tasks that need to be performed and determines those which, if there is a delay at any stage, would cause a delay in the completion date of the project as a whole.

This critical path also identifies activities which can be simultaneously carried out. Its applications throughout the business include the following:

- Launching of a new store
- New product launch
- Automation of the production process
- Business relocation
- Effective marketing campaign

The CPA is a visual tool and is a technique that shows all the activities which are needed for a project to be duly completed, and the best order that they can be completed in.

It is vital for project managers to understand which activities depend on the completion of an earlier activity in order for it to be completed.

Nodes which are drawn in circles are used to represent the activities. Each node shows three numbers including:

- Node number – which represents the order in which it was drawn
- Earliest start time – the time by which the previous activity needs to be completed.
- Latest finish time –the earliest the next activity can commence

| Component | Description |
|---|---|
| Node | A circle that represents a point in time where an activity is started or finished. The node (circle) is split into three sections: <br><br> The left half of the circle is the unique node (activity) number – the network diagram draws these in order <br><br> The top right section shows the earliest start time **(EST)** that an activity can commence based on the completion of the previous activity <br><br> The bottom right section shows the latest finish time **(LFT)** by which the previous activity must be completed |
| Activities | An activity is something that takes time. An activity is shown on the network as a line, linking the nodes (circles). A description of the activity, or a letter representing the activity, is usually shown above the relevant line |
| Duration | The length of time it takes to complete an activity – shown as a number of the relevant units (e.g. hours, days) under the activity line |

The CPA has several benefits and setbacks in its applications:

- Firstly, it allows for the more efficient use of resources
- Secondly, it is a great tool for monitoring, planning and decision-making

An example of a CPA is as follows:

| Task | Activity | Order | Duration (months) |
|---|---|---|---|
| A | Conduct customer research | Starting activity | 2 |
| B | Design product concept | Begin when A complete | 4 |
| C | Design and test product prototype | Begin when B complete | 2 |
| D | Develop and test production tooling | Begin when C complete | 3 |
| E | Notify suppliers of requirements | Begin when C complete | 1 |
| F | Commence production | Begin when D complete | 3 |
| G | Conduct launch promotion | Begin when F complete | 1 |

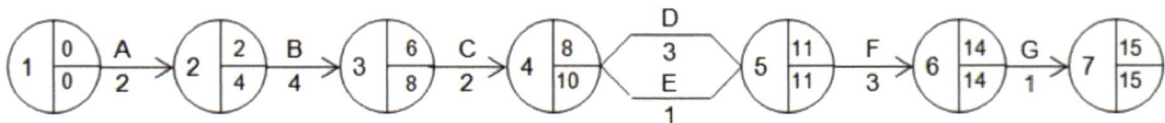

Limitations of CPA are the high reliance on estimates, and hence these estimates need to be reliable in order for the right results to be achieved. CPA does not guarantee the success of a project and resources may not be as flexible as management would like them to be.

## Self-assessment questions

1) Discuss the financial strategies and accounts which are used by business
2) Explain how a business can align its financial objectives to its corporate objectives
3) Give examples of how financial data can be used to measure and assess performance
4) Define a published account. What are its main features?
5) How can a business utilise its financial strategies in making investment decisions?

## Topic 3.4 - Influences on Business Decisions

### Learning Outcome

The aim of this section is for students to understand the following:

- Corporate Influences
- Corporate Culture
- Shareholders versus Stakeholders
- Business Ethics

**Corporate Influences**

A business strategy which is considered to be 'short-termism' is where the focus is on a quick financial reward and profits, this can be high risk. A business strategy that is focused on investment in research and development, new technology and staff development is considered to be 'long-termism'.

Long-termism is arguably the more commercially prudent approach to a business strategy that incorporates Corporate Social Responsibility (CSR) and ethical behaviour.

A business also needs to consider decision-making and explore if this is evidence based or subjective. Evidence based decision-making approaches are quantitative, such as decision trees and critical path analysis and can be evaluated. Whereas subjective decision-making is taken by key individuals in the organisation, and may be considered by a 'gut feeling', which can be risky.

A small business may have the attributes of a short-term strategy and subjective decision-making, due to a lack of resources. A small business is likely to make a loss in the first months of business, due to high start-up costs and inexperience.

**Corporate Culture**

Corporate culture can be difficult to define and understand; a statement such as 'the way we do things around here' is probably a good definition of culture. Other factors to consider are that 'culture' is the shared values of the business, the beliefs and norms of the business, and the typical day-to-day behaviour of the business.

Corporate culture can be defined as strong or weak; the characteristics of a strong culture are:

- Consistent behaviour of staff
- Staff understanding and responding to the culture
- Policies and procedures are not required
- Culture is embedded
- The characteristics of a weak culture are:
- Inconsistent staff behaviour
- Extensive policies, procedures and bureaucracy
- Little alignment to business values

The classifications of corporate culture are:

- Power culture – this is where the power of the organisation is held by a few individuals, and that influence spreads throughout the organisation. A power culture has few rules and regulations with a consequence of quick decision-making that is not in the long-term best interest of the organisation.
- Role culture – this is where the business is highly controlled with rules, Individuals know their role and what their responsibilities are. The organisational structure is bureaucratic with numerous management layers, and decision-making is very slow.
- Task Culture – this is where staff teams are formed to address a specific project or resolve a problem. Power will shift in the organisation as the task is given priority.
- Person Culture – this is where individuals see themselves as unique and superior in the organisation. This type of culture is seen where there are a lot of professionals in one organisation such as lawyers or accountants.

There is not a right or wrong corporate culture, as this often depends on the background of the organisation and the strength and clarity of the organisation's founder. The vision and direction that the management want the business to follow and also the types of products or services that the business offers, will determine the culture. The culture can evolve and change as the businesses focus, staff or products/services change.

There can be difficulties in changing an established culture as it may be well embedded, be normal custom and practice and seen as the normal way to work. This can led staff to become resistant to change. They may be concerned that it will impact on them negatively, such as on their working conditions or affect pay. Any changes need to be managed effectively through good communication and consultation with all staff.

Some examples of corporate cultures in an organisation are:

- Ikea – a consistent culture among employees who embrace the values of the organisation.
- NHS – public sector organisation that has complex cultural challenges.
- John Lewis - employees are shareholders with a common interest in the company's fortunes

**Shareholders v Stakeholders**

A stakeholder is someone who has a vested interest in the organisation's activities and decision-making. A stakeholder may be the owner of the business, customers, financial providers (bank), local community, employees etc. A shareholder is someone who has a financial stake in the organisation and is interested in dividend pay outs.

Stakeholders will have corporate objectives which are long-term investments in the business, whereas a shareholder may have corporate objectives which are short-term and concerned with making a profit. This can lead to conflict within the organisation. (The John Lewis example above, however, where the employees are shareholders, would dispute this.)

In order to be successful businesses need to take into consideration all of their stakeholders and their interests financial or otherwise in the business. Failure to do this can alienate certain stakeholders and impact on the businesses ability to succeed. It is about getting the balance between financial reward and meeting other stakeholder's needs.

**Business Ethics**

Ethics are the moral rights and wrongs of a decision taken by the management of a business. Organisations have ethical policies as they believe in this value judgement or that this policy will improve the credibility of the business and encourage more customers to purchase their products.

Ethical policies may include a greener organisation by reducing pollution, disposal of waste in a more environmentally friendly way, sponsoring local community events and fair trade products. Organisations such as The Body Shop and the Co-Op have strong ethical policies.

A business needs to weigh up the cost and the benefit of employing business ethics and the impact that it may have on profit and market share, when making decisions. Being an ethically renowned business can give the company an edge, a USP and have a positive impact on profits, however, there may be additional costs.

Corporate Social Responsibility (CSR) is closely linked to ethical policies but differs in that CSR is concerned with responsibility to stakeholders where ethics is morally correct behaviour.

**Activity 49 –**

Log onto the internet and read the article on the Body Shop ethics.
http://www.thebodyshop.co.uk/values/index.aspx

# Topic 3.5 - Assessing Competitiveness

## Learning Outcome

The aim of this section is for students to understand the following:

- Interpretation of Financial Statements
- Ratio Analysis
- Human Resources

## Interpretation of Financial Statements

An international standard for public accounts has been defined by the International Accounting Standards Committee (IASC). This framework has the objective of ensuring financial statements provide information which are of benefit to different users and stakeholders who need to use such information to make informed economic decisions. These financial statements are published accounts of businesses, and include the income statement and balance sheet. These are used by managers, lenders, potential investors and government, just to mention a few. Below is an example of the financial statements of XYZ Plc.

*Income statement and balance sheet for XYZ Plc as of 31 December 2009:*

| Income statement | | Balance sheet | | |
|---|---|---|---|---|
| | | | £m | £m |
| | £m | | | |
| Revenue | 1350 | Non-current assets: | | |
| Cost of sales | (570) | Plant, equipment and property | | 4050 |
| Gross Profit | 780 | Current assets: | | |
| | | Inventories | 40 | |
| | | Trade receivables | 160 | |
| | | Cash and cash equivalents | 80 | |
| Other Expenses | (260) | Total current assets: | 280 | |
| Operating profit | 520 | Current liabilities | | |
| | | Trade payables | (220) | |
| | | Net current liabilities | | 60 |
| | | Non-current liabilities | | |
| | | Bank loans | | (1854) |
| | | Net Assets | | 2256 |
| | | Equity | | |
| | | Share Capital | 950 | |
| | | Retained profits and reserves | 1306 | |
| | | Total equity | | 2256 |
| Notes to accounts: | | | | |
| Total dividend for the year was £350m.<br>Purchases on credit in the year were £850m<br>All sales are made on credit.<br>Market share price on 31 December 2008 was £11.11 | | | | |

The above financial information will provide the basis for the financial information used throughout to calculate the accounting ratios.

**Understanding Financial Objectives**

Financial objectives are the goals which revolve around the fiscal aspirations of the business. These will be set within a specific time period, usually a financial year.

Financial objectives need to be set to provide targets for the business and to measure the level of business performance.

Financial objectives are often set and reviewed annually and have a very important role in the greater strategic vision of the business. For instance, large businesses have their main objective of increasing the return for their shareholder. They set financial objectives often quarterly and then yearly, and tend to have five-year financial objectives to keep the business focused and maintain its vision.

Cash-flow targets are a significant part of any financial objectives strategy. A business must be fully aware of the opportunity cost of cash-flow. In other words, there is always a trade-off between having too much cash and not enough.

Cost minimisation is a process which aims to reduce costs which the business accrues. A business will attempt to minimise its costs in order to maximise its profit margin.

Cost minimisation examines areas where savings can be made. Furthermore, it could result in cost-effective measures like reduction of staff employed and change of suppliers, or a relocation of premises.

The Return on Capital Employed (ROCE) targets measures the business returns in a given time period.

ROCE is an expression of the operating profit as a percentage of the amount of capital utilised in the business otherwise known as the amount of capital employed. It measures the profitability of the firm and its performance.

ROCE targets enable the business to set what it considers to be the minimum percentage return which it expects on its total investments.

Shareholders' return is seen as the major financial objective of any business. This ensures the shareholders are kept satisfied with the performance of the business.

Two major elements of shareholders' return are the dividend paid and the market value of the share itself.

**Ratio Analysis**

**Return on Capital**

The return on capital is a measure of the net effect of an investment in the business on its profit and overall efficiency.

Businesses always expect that when they make an investment, that investment will yield a positive return.

The formula for return on capital is:

$$\text{Return on capital} \quad = \quad \frac{\underline{\text{Non-current liabilities}}}{\text{Total Equity}} \quad \text{x 100}$$

For example, a business makes an investment of £35000 on machinery. It figures out that this would lead to sales increase of an extra £12,000. Hence the return on capital (ROC) is

$$\text{Return on capital} \quad = \quad \frac{\underline{£12000}}{£35000} \quad \text{x} \quad 100$$

$$\text{Return on capital} \quad = \quad 34.3\%$$

**Using Financial Data to Measure and Assess Performance**

Financial data is produced by a company on an annual basis, and it shows the performance of the business within the previous financial year as set against earlier years.

The annual report is produced and given to the shareholders, and it is of vital importance to all stakeholders, but particularly banks, employees and potential and current investors.

An income statement shows the summary of the trading activity of the business including its expenditures usually during the course of the financial year. In addition to annual reports, there are also mid-year statements produced. The profitability or loss-making activities are shown in this statement.

Gross profit is the profit which the business makes after the sales costs have been deducted but before any other expenses are taken into account. The operating profit is the profit made after the other expenses are taken into account and deducted.

Gross profit margin is expressed in a percentage and is the ratio of the gross profit to the sales revenue. Hence:

$$\text{Gross profit margin \%} = \frac{\text{Gross profit}}{\text{Revenue}} \times 100$$

Profit Quality is the degree to which the profit figures can be sustained over a period of time in the near future.

Profit utilisation is the way that the profit which the business makes is used. It is the split between the dividend and reinvested capital.

## Balance sheet analysis

The balance sheet is used to display the net worth of a business. It details both the asset and liabilities of the business. Assets are what the business owns, and liabilities are what the business owes to others. Assets could be current or non-current assets. Other assets include fixed and intangible assets.

Liabilities could be current or non-current liabilities. In both cases, assets and liabilities could be looked at in terms of net assets and net current liabilities.

Working capital is used to reflect the ability of the firm to fulfil its daily expense obligations.

Depreciation is the loss in value of fixed assets over a period of time. For example, a van owned by the company will be used over several years, and over that period its value will inevitably decline. The actual value and worth on the balance sheet should be a true reflection of the actual value of the fixed asset at a given time.

The gearing ratio is used to show the level of borrowing of the business, and thus by implication how the business could be affected by changes in interest rates. Heavy gearing makes it more complex in terms of producing accurate budgets and cash flows.

When a business has low 'trade payables' from its creditors, it would be worth considering whether it could improve the working capital and in-flow of cash through the negotiation of a better deal with its suppliers.

When 'trade receivables' of the business from its debtors is high, this could be because of fierce competition; the business might need to look at more competitive credit terms to have a solid competitive advantage. Otherwise, it could due to weaknesses within the business.

## Using financial data

The financial data of a business is important for both the stakeholders of the business and internal purposes.

- Trend Analysis - The analysis of trends and tracking performance of the business over a period of time is achieved through the use of the financial data of the business
- Inter-firm comparisons - Comparisons between different firms are used to understand the competitors, similar firms and businesses of the same size. This enables benchmarking against performances of other firms to gauge current performance and strengthening the position of the business. This is known as inter-firm comparison. Intra-firm comparisons within the business include division, branch, and geographical location comparisons of the business. It also includes comparisons between the product ranges of the business. Ultimately the purpose of such exercise would be to improve the overall performance of the business
- Decision-making - The processes of decision-making which pertain to the direction of the firm are influenced by the financial status of the firm. This could be investing in new machinery and equipment or employees
- Financial data trends - Financial data tend to be published for public use. It provides vital information about the business. These are published accounts and are audited independently to verify the accuracy of the information provided. However, there are tendencies of businesses to falsify and over-exaggerate positive figures

## Activity 50 – Define gross profit margin.

**Liquidity ratios**

Liquidity ratios are used to measure the ability of the firm to meet its daily expenses by comparing the current liabilities and assets of the business. Such comparisons are important in assessing if the business is viable in the short term.

The acid test ratio and current ratio are the two frequently used liquidity tests.

Acid test ratio is the difference between the current assets and inventories expressed as a ratio to the current liabilities. That is:

$$\text{Acid test ratio} = \frac{(\text{Current assets} - \text{Inventories})}{\text{Current liabilities}}$$

Hence at XYZ Plc, the acid test ratio is:

$$\text{Acid test ratio} = \frac{(280 - 40)}{220}$$

$$\text{Acid test ratio} = \frac{240}{220}$$

$$\text{Acid test ratio} = 1: 1.09$$

Therefore, for every £1 of current liabilities it has £1.09 of in current assets which excludes the inventories.

Current ratio is also known as the working capital ratio:

$$\text{Current ratio} = \frac{\text{Current assets}}{\text{Current liabilities}}$$

Hence at XYZ Plc, the current ratio is:

$$\text{Current ratio} = \frac{280}{220}$$

Current ratio = 1:1.27

Therefore, for every £1 of current liabilities, XYZ plc has £1.27 in the current assets.

## Profitability ratios

Profitability ratios are used by the business to analyse the profits of the firm in relation to either its trading performance, hence the capital utilised in generating profit or the revenue from sales.

The return on capital employed (ROCE) and the operating profit margin are the two frequently used liquidity tests.

The return on capital employed (ROCE) is the primary efficiency, and it shows the overall performance of the business expressed as a percentage of the total long-term capital invested into it.

The ROCE also measures the level of efficiency of the business in managing its capital and how it uses this capital in generation of profit.

$$\text{ROCE \%} = \frac{\text{Operating profit}}{\text{Capital Employed}} \times 100$$

Hence for XYZ plc, this is:

$$\text{ROCE \%} = \frac{520}{(280 + 4050)} \times 100$$

$$\text{ROCE \%} = \frac{520}{4330} \times 100$$

$$\text{ROCE \%} = 12.01\%$$

Therefore, for every £1 of invested capital, a profit of 0.1201p is made.

This figure is then compared with past results and performance of competitors, to gauge the actual level of profitability.

Operating Profit Margin is used to show the relationship between the operating profit and sales revenue:

$$\text{Operating profit margin \%} = \frac{\text{Operating profit}}{\text{Revenue}} \times 100$$

Hence at XYZ plc, this is:

$$\text{Operating profit margin \%} = \frac{520}{1350} \times 100$$

$$\text{Operating profit margin \%} = 38.52\%$$

This shows that for every £1 of sales and after the deduction of expenses, 38.5p of profit is left.

**Activity 51 – Would you consider this to be a good operating profit margin?**

**Financial efficiency ratios**

These are predominantly used internally to assess the efficiency of management in handling the financial operations of the business.

- Stock or inventory turnover
- Receivables (debtor) days
- Asset turnover
- Payables (creditor) days

**Stock or inventory turnover** is used to measure the ratio of the cost of sales to the inventory; hence:

$$\text{Stock turnover} = \frac{\text{Cost of sales}}{\text{Inventory}}$$

Hence at XYZ plc:

$$\text{Stock turnover} = \frac{\text{Cost of sales}}{\text{Inventory}}$$

$$\text{Stock turnover} = \frac{570}{40}$$

$$\text{Stock turnover} = 14.3$$

This means that 14.3 times more inventory is sold by the business per year. In other words, it holds inventories for less than one month on average.

**Receivables (debtor) days** are used to measure the average number of days which it takes to receive payments from customers.

$$\text{Receivables (debtor) days} = \frac{\text{(Receivables x 365 days)}}{\text{Revenue}}$$

At XYZ plc:

$$\text{Receivables (debtor) days} = \frac{\text{(160 x 365)}}{1350}$$

$$\text{Receivables (debtor) days} = 43 \text{ days}$$

XYZ plc can expect to receive payment 43 days after the sale of the product.

**Asset turnover** is used to measure the efficiency of the assets which the business uses to generate sales revenue.

$$\text{Asset turnover} = \frac{\text{Sales}}{\text{Net Assets}}$$

At XYZ plc:

$$\text{Asset turnover} = \frac{1350}{2256}$$

$$\text{Asset turnover} = 0.598$$

This shows that for every £1 a sale of 0.59p was generated by the business.

**Payables (creditor) days** measure the average amount of time taken to pay suppliers for goods purchased on credit. It is expressed in days:

$$\text{Payables (creditor) days} = \frac{\text{(Payables x 365 days)}}{\text{Credit purchases}}$$

At XYZ plc:

$$\text{Payables (creditor) days} = \frac{\text{(220 x 365)}}{\text{Credit purchases}}$$

**Gearing ratio** is used to measure the percentage of the capital of a firm which is financed by long-term loans and compulsory interest bearing sources that the company has to pay interest on, irrespective of profit.

$$\text{Gearing ratio \%} = \frac{\text{Non-current liabilities}}{\text{Capital Employed}}$$

At XYZ plc:

$$\text{Gearing ratio \%} = \frac{1854}{4330}$$

$$\text{Gearing ratio \%} = 0.43$$

Hence for every £1invested in the business, 43p is from a long-term debt liability with compulsory interest rate payments.

**Activity 52 – What is gearing and what are its advantages and disadvantages?**

**Shareholder ratios**

**Shareholder ratios** measure the value of return to the shareholder.

Dividend per share (DPS) is the total number of dividends divided by the number of issued shares.

$$\text{Dividend per share (DPS)} = \frac{\text{Total dividend}}{\text{Number of issued shares}}$$

At XYZ Plc:

$$\text{Dividend per share (DPS)} = \frac{\pounds 350m}{950} = 36.8p$$

Therefore the shareholder will receive 36.8 p per share held.

**Dividend yield** is a measure of the dividend received as a rate of return when in comparison to the current market share price.

$$\text{Dividend yield} = \frac{\text{Dividend per share}}{\text{Market share price}} \times 100$$

At XYZ plc:

$$\text{Dividend yield} = \frac{0.368}{11.11} \times 100$$

$$\text{Dividend yield} = 3.3\%$$

Hence, if a £1 dividend were received, then the expected value of the share would be £3.30.

**Value and limitations of ratio analysis**

Ratio analysis can be a vital tool for measuring performance of the business. However, these can be inaccurate, especially when the financial data is not a true representation of the actual financial situation of the business.

Furthermore ratio analysis only uses financial data and does not take into consideration other aspects of the business.

**Human Resources**

Overall, human resource objectives are designed to help ensure the success of the business. It will include: the optimum usage of the potential of the workforce; matching skills with the needs of the business; ensuring the maintenance of a workforce that suits the needs of the business; maintaining strong employee-employer relations; having a strategic location base for the workforce and reduction in the cost of labour.

Influences on the HR objectives can be:

- Internal - Internal influences include the alignment of the human resources objectives with the marketing and production strategies respectively. Furthermore, the corporate objectives could affect HR objectives because of aspirations to achieve goals which include market share growth, increased outlook of business on its competitiveness and increase in shareholder returns
- External - External factors that influence HR decisions include government legislation and requirements; shortage and intense competition for highly skilled workers; changes in the economy and technological change

**Activity 53 – Do you think redundancies can be part of an HR strategy?**

**HR management**

There are different approaches to HR management:

- Hard HR Management
- Soft HR Management

Hard HR Management uses judgemental systems of appraisal, minimum wage levels, fixed-term contracts, tall organisational structures, recruitment through external sources and limited delegation of authority.

Benefits of this type of management include:

- Strengthening of competitive advantage
- Minimal expenditure on training and development
- Positive links between wages and quantity produced by employees

The weaknesses of this system include:

- Lack of empowerment as a result of limited delegation
- Difficulty in retaining new employees
- Minimal attention to needs of employees

Soft HR management is based on the notion of employees as the most beneficial asset of the business. It focuses on promotion within the business, flat structure of the organisation, effective appraisal systems and training and development opportunities for the employees.

Benefits of this type of management include:

- High rates of employee retention
- Reduced recruitment costs
- Training and development opportunities which enable employees to fulfil personal and corporate goals
- Reward systems which encourage work and creativity at a consistently high standard

The weaknesses of this system include:

- A strong reliance on an organisational culture of long-term training and development commitment
- Uncertain relationship with trade unions, often resulting in tensions

**Activity 54 – Think of a business you are familiar with. Which HR strategy do they employ? Is it effective?**

Developing and Implementing Workforce Plans

Workforce planning ensures that the HR objectives are achieved. There are a number of elements which are vital when drawing up a plan for the workforce. Below is a workforce planning cycle. In drawing up a workforce plan, the following factors need to be considered:

- Labour turnover data
- Government initiatives and directives from the EU on workforce practices and conditions
- Skills audit of current workforce
- Data from market research

Benefits of workforce plans include:

- Facilitation of favourable working plans
- Organisational success that is dependent on the right mix of employees
- Efficient workforce utilisation to reduce costs to the business long-term
- Getting the right people in the right job with the right skills

Workforce plans are influenced by internal and external factors:

- Internal factors include production objectives, finance, corporate objectives and marketing objectives
- External factors include trend of the labour markets, competition, new technology and buyer behaviour and market trends

In the implantation of workforce plans, several issues must be considered, including:

- Cost
- Training
- Employer-employee relations
- Corporate image
- Retention rates

These have positive and negative effects on the business and the plans to achieve corporate objectives. The value of workforce plans cannot be underestimated. When efficiently implemented they lead to the enhancement of business efficiency.

**Competitive Organisational Structures**

Organisations change their structure, sometimes fairly frequently, to adjust to changing market conditions.

In large organisations there are several structural types which include the matrix structure, bureaucratic and entrepreneurial structures.

The structure of the organisation has several effects on competitiveness of the business. This is reflected through:

- Effectiveness of the channels of communication
- The personnel in the business are involved in decision making
- Efficiency of business operations and cost minimisation
- Speed at which strategic decisions are made

Due to the importance of competitiveness, the business will adapt its activities to improve its competitiveness. This can be achieved through:

- Decentralisation
- De-layering
- Centralisation
- Outsourcing
- Home working
- Flexible workforce

**Effective Employer-Employee Relations**

Communication is of fundamental importance to any business, either large or small. It is of particular importance in terms of maintaining good employer-employee relations. Effective communication leads to improved change management, greater motivation and identification of culture and loyalty to the organisation by employee.

Communication can be improved through improving the skills of the employees in various communication techniques, and in establishing the needs of the employees before making changes to existing methods of communication.

Employee representation is used to facilitate the speed of decision-making on behalf of the employees. These could be accomplished through the use of: work councils, employee groups or Trade Unions.

Employee representation is important because it involves employees having a say in the business, and for managers it can be vital in resolving issues that the workforce have, thus enabling the business to keep a happy and productive workforce.

The drawback is that employee representation takes time, and it tends to lengthen any decision-making process which involves the workforce. Furthermore, managers can feel undermined, and this can result in distrust and resentment towards employees. Industrial disputes may arise which lead to friction between employer and employee relations. To resolve such scenarios, the following actions can be used:

- Dialogue and discussion
- Arbitration
- Incorporating alternative methods of resolution of problems in employee contracts
- Conciliation

**Self-assessment questions**

1) Outline the processes of implementing human resource strategies.

2) Distinguish between HR objectives and HR strategies.

3) Explain the ways in which a business can develop and implement its workforce plans.

4) Describe the nature of competitive organisational structures.

5) What is the importance of effective employer-employee relations?

**Topic 3.6 - Managing Change**

**Learning Outcome**

The aim of this section is for students to understand the following:

- Causes and Effects of Change
- Key Factors in Change
- Scenario Planning

**Internal Causes of Change**

Change is inevitable in business. It takes place for several reasons which include:

- A desire to expand and increase market share
- A desire to grow overseas
- Technological changes
- A move to a new sector or industry
- A major acquisition or take-over
- Changes in legislation

Change is also used as an avenue to increase the economies of scale of a business.

Business growth can be both internal and external. The former is the business expansion through the opening of new shops, branches and facilities; the latter is the expansion of the business through the means of take-overs and mergers of another business within or outside its industry.

Integration and synergy are effective ways of increasing the growth of the business depending on its specific needs and objectives. Several types of integration include:

- Vertical backward integration
- Conglomerate integration
- Vertical forward integration
- Horizontal integration

It is common for a business to wish to reduce the size of its workforce in order to reduce its overheads. This results in retrenchment and down-sizing of the workforce.

Internal changes can occur through the change of ownership of a firm. This could be through:

- Management buyouts
- Sale of the business to employees
- Passing on the business to the next generation
- Floatation of the business on the stock exchange
- A take-over by another company

Internal change also occurs through poor performance of the business. This is usually based on persistent levels of failure within the business and the reporting of losses to the business.

In order to salvage and resuscitate the business, the business would need to experience internal change.

Private equity ownerships have been used to facilitate internal change of underperforming businesses in recent years. In this case, the business is bought by wealthy investors who seek to change the performance of its management.

It should be noted that private equity-owned businesses are not listed on the stock exchange.

**Scenario Planning**

Planning for change is important simply because change is inevitable, and needs to be managed properly if it is to be successful. Corporate plans are made by the business to ensure that methodical approaches to planning are made which would have details of the central objectives of the organisation and the steps which it needs to take to achieve them.

Corporate plans include the following:

- Strategies of the business to achieve these objectives
- Overall organisational objectives including sales growth, profit target and market share growth
- Department objectives of the key areas of the business and the link with the overall corporate objective

Below is a diagram showing the linkage of corporate plans to its strategies and objectives:

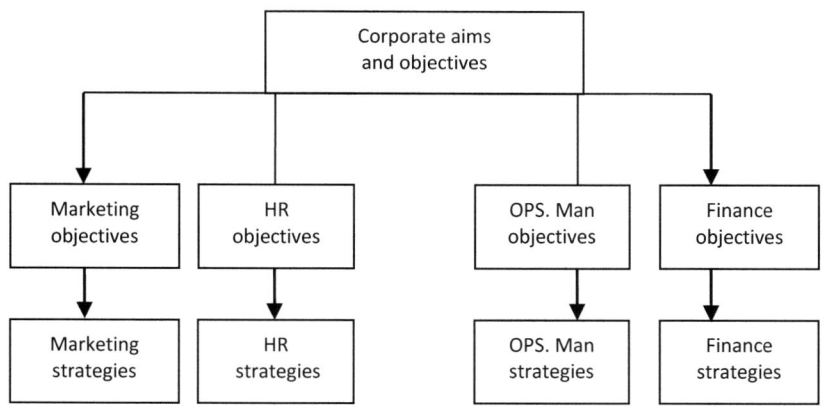

Corporate planning enables the business to have a clear focus and direction.

Through corporate planning, the senior management can evaluate the strengths and weaknesses of a business and formulate a strategy for maximising the former and minimising the latter. Corporate plans are of immensely high value to the following stakeholders:

- Lenders and creditors of the business
- Members of staff who can identify with the objectives of the business
- Potential investors
- Government bodies

The influences on corporate plans can be external or internal. External influences include actions of competitors, changes in the economic policies, macro-economic conditions and technological changes.

Internal influences on corporate plans include the operating capacity of the business, organisational culture, availability of financial resources, expertise and managerial skills of the key personnel of the business and the size of the workforce.

Contingency Planning is used by the business to prepare for any unforeseen events. It is known as business continuity planning. It is used by the business to minimise the potential impacts of an unforeseen event, and ideally takes necessary measures to prevent such occurrences. It follows a methodical approach through:

- Identification of potential disasters
- Assessment of the likelihood of such disasters actually occurring
- Minimisation of the potential impact of such disasters on the business
- Making adequate provision for continuity of the business after such a crisis arises

**Risk Management**

This is identifying what the risks of something going wrong are, identifying them and putting a plan in place to deal with the risks. Organisations prepare risk assessments in order to have a contingency plan in place in the event of a natural disaster, IT systems failure or the loss of key staff. The aim is to ensure business continuity in the event of something going wrong and to have succession planning incorporated into the HR strategy to train other staff that have high potential in the event of key staff leaving the organisation.

The decision makers in an organisation will have an influence on what they consider to be an acceptable risk for the business. Examples of risk mitigation are:

- Risk Acceptance – this is where the cost of mitigation is greater than the cost of risk itself
- Risk Avoidance – this is pulling out of the risk altogether
- Risk Limitation – this is a common risk strategy where a contingency plan is in place
- Risk Transference – this is transferring the risk to a third party, to outsource the operations of the organisation
- In some businesses risk taking is encouraged and failure is tolerated in exchange for big rewards next time. The focus is on maximising the potential returns on each risk

**Key Influences on the Change Process: Leadership**

Strong leadership is an essential element in the business. This is because of the influence of effective leadership on the business and its ability to oversee the objectives of the business and execution of the corporate plans. Quality leadership involves the following key components:

- Ensuring business focus on achievement of goals and objectives
- Motivation and inspiration of workforce
- Enabling full potential realisation of members of the organisation
- Exertion of positive influence on others

Effectiveness of leadership involves the ability of the leader to think critically, ability to communicate, determination to succeed, great self-motivation and the willingness to listen.

Styles of leadership include the following:

- Democratic leadership
- Laissez-faire leadership
- Autocratic leadership
- Bureaucratic leadership
- Paternalistic leadership

Douglas McGregor's theory of motivation identified the theory X and theory Y concept of motivation.

Theory X concept is based on the view that the employees are lazy and would avoid work. Therefore, close supervision is imperative. Hence theory X managers are viewed to as authoritarian.

The theory Y concept identifies workers as ambitious and highly motivated by self. Hence theory Y managers need to facilitate the work environment to such a standard that enables such workers to thrive and supersede their ambition and drive.

Factors that influence styles of leadership include both external and internal factors. External factors include legal changes, economic environment and the speed and nature of change in the industry.

Internal factors that affect the influence of leadership style include the natural or preferred style of the leader, the time limit, experience and skills level of the team, and the amount of work involved.

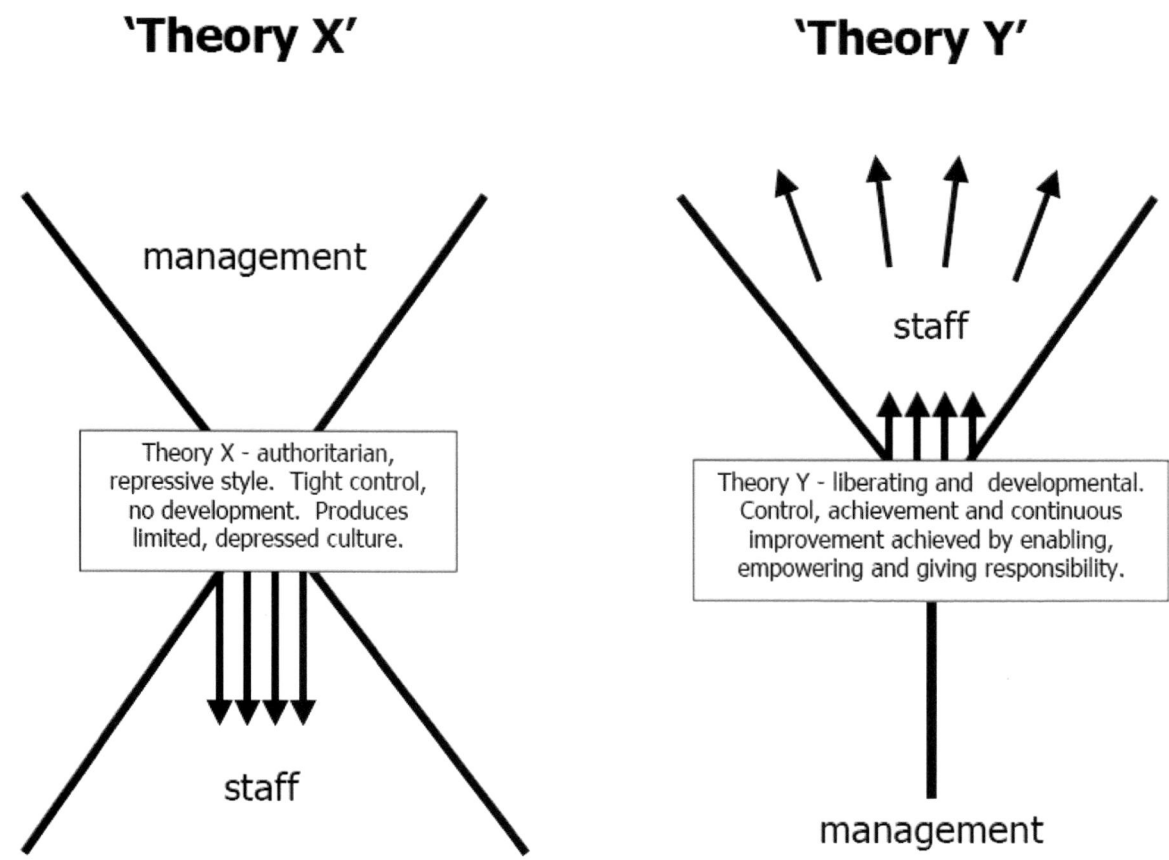

**Key Influences on the Change Process: Culture**

The culture of any organisation is unique to that organisation. It is an attribute which describes the way the people within the organisation view the world and respond to it as they strive to achieve certain goals. Organisational culture varies from one organisation to another, and can be either positive to the business, or negative.

Types of organisational culture include the:

- Role culture
- Entrepreneurial culture
- Task culture
- Power culture
- Person culture

It is sometimes necessary to undertake a programme to change the culture of an organisation for a number of potential reasons:

- The current culture is deemed unhealthy
- There is a merger or take-over of the business
- Responses to changing market conditions in order to maximise the products and services of the company
- Declining profits and market share
- Demotivation of employees
- External (perhaps governmental) pressure

There are always problems with trying to change an organisations culture. This is because at the heart of such changes are the requirement to change people, and people are almost always resistant to change.

Employees will usually see an attempt to change culture as being a negative statement about them - perhaps that they are not working hard enough - and therefore will be automatically resistant.

There are six essential points to consider which ensure successful change in organisational culture:

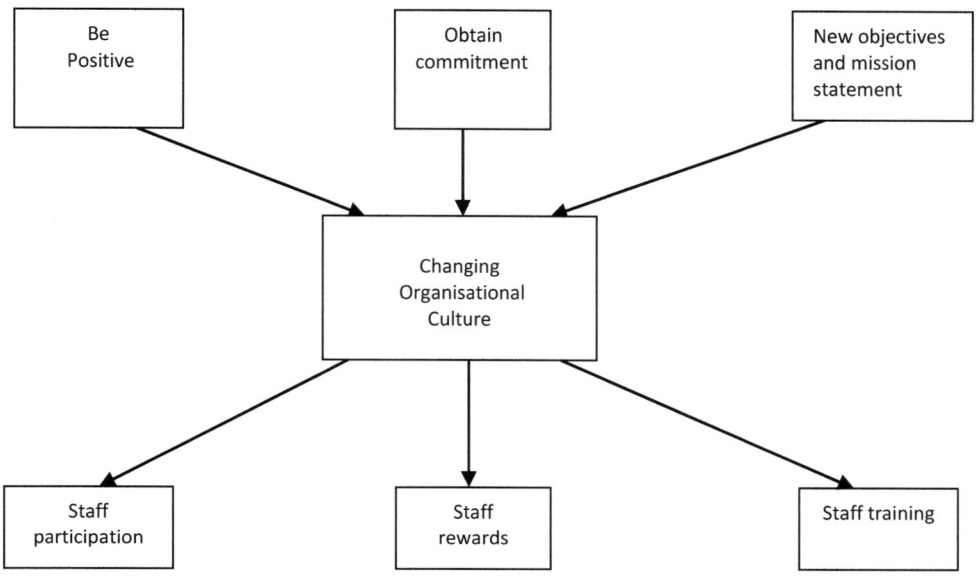

Organisational culture is very important in a business. Hence in order for it to be successful, it must evaluate its perceptions and attitude which determine its outlook and ultimately its success.

**Activity 55 – Why do you think change is inevitable, and why does it need to be managed?**

**Making Strategic Decisions**

The strategic plan for a business is the long-term plan of where you want the business to be at a given point in the future. The process of decision-making in the business could be either strategic or tactical.

Tactical decisions have the following characteristics:

- It is often within one department and not the whole organisation
- It is reversible when unsuccessful
- It has consequences in the short-term
- Taken at middle management
- Utilises fewer resources

Strategic decisions have the following characteristics:

- It is hard to reverse
- Utilises numerous resources
- It is usually long-term
- Taken at senior management
- It is often with the whole organisation

Importance of information management

Information management is about obtaining the relevant information from the best source within the organisation at the right time. The term Management Information System (MIS) is used when such information has been successfully recorded and collated through the use of information technology in order for the decision-making process to be done.

The purpose of an effective MIS is to provide senior managers with the following:

- Simulated results of the impact of taking a decision on the performance of the business
- Data about options which would enable more accurate choices to be made
- Provision of up-to-date information on the performance of the individual products and profit centres

Strategic choice, strategy implementation and strategic analysis are the three main stages in making strategic decisions for the business. This is also known as scientific decision-making.

**Activity 56 – What do you think could be the consequences to a business of a poor MIS?**

**Implementing and Managing Change**

We have noted several times the importance to every business of change management. Change management involves the ability of the firm to cope with major changes which are gradual long-term or one-off changes.

Business process re-engineering occurs when a revolutionary and often dramatic change in the business occurs which is unanticipated and results in wholesale vital changes. Incremental or evolutionary changes take place over a long-term period and can be anticipated or dramatic. Factors which cause changes to take place include:

- Legal changes
- Technological changes
- Actions of competitors in the business
- Macroeconomic changes

Communication is vital at every stage of change management; decisions and ideas need to be communicated effectively if the change programme is to be successful.

## Force field analysis

This concept was created by Kurt Lewin and is used to provide a framework for analysis of the forces, either for or against, which influence a change programme. It involves the following steps:

- Outlining of a change proposal
- Making a two-column list – with the forces of change in one column and the forces against in the second column
- Assigning an estimate score for each force – 5 being the strongest and 1 being the weakest

A project champion should be appointed by the senior management team to take charge of any change programme. These should be employees who are influential and motivational and can inspire others to "buy-in" to the desired changes.

A project group could also be established to bring together people from different departments or functions that have different perspectives and expertise.

John Kotter identified an eight-stage process of promoting change. This is outlined below:

- The establishment of a sense of urgency
- Creation of an effective project team to lead the change
- Development of a vision and strategy for change
- Communication of the change vision
- Empowerment of people to take action
- The generation of short-term gains from change that benefits numerous people
- Consolidation of these gains and production of even greater change
- Building change into the culture of the organisation in order to make this a natural process

It should be noted that as there are proponents for change in an organisation, there are also opponents of change.

The reasons for resisting change include a lack of trust, fear of failure, false beliefs about the need for change, inertia, unwillingness to venture into the unknown, and loss of value.

The importance of these resistance factors varies between organisations and businesses.

**Self-assessment questions**

1) How does a business ensure due management of change?
2) Highlight the internal causes of change.
3) Outline the necessary steps to be taken when planning for change.
4) What are the key factors which influence the change process culture?
5) Give five reasons why a business needs to make strategic decisions.

**Activity 57 –**

Log onto the internet and read the article on business leadership.

http://www.theguardian.com/sustainable-business/transformational-leadership-key-self-doubt

Log onto the internet and read the article on Nokia failing to change.
http://fortune.com/2013/05/08/why-corporate-giants-fail-to-change

# Theme 4

# Global Business

Topic 4.1 - Globalisation

Topic 4.2 - Global Markets and Business Expansion

Topic 4.3 - Global Marketing

Topic 4.4 - Global Industries and Companies (multinational corporations)

**Topic 4.1 - Globalisation**

**Learning Outcome**

The aim of this section is for students to understand the following:

- Growing Economies
- International Trade and Business Growth
- Factors Contributing to Increased Globalisation
- Protectionism
- Trading Blocs

## Globalisation

Globalisation can be defined as the process of shaping the lives of people across national borders as a direct result of development across the globe.

Through the process of globalisation, there is the free movement of goods and services and trade across international boundaries, devoid of any barriers that may have previously constituted a hindrance to their free movement across national boundaries. Therefore, it has made capital, goods and services as well as technology move freely between international economies. The movement of labour has also been facilitated as it becomes easier to cross national boundaries in search of favourable employment opportunities.

Globalisation is caused by:

- Communication improvements
- Increase in multi-national corporations across the globe.
- Changes in technology

Governments have co-operated together to ensure that there are favourable conditions which are created to facilitate the global movement with limited restrictions. Inter-governmental alliances have succeeded in minimising the existence of tariffs and trade barriers.

Within the European Union, there has been the formation of the single Euro currency which has made it possible to have a single European market.

Positive consequences of globalisation:

- Efficient technological transfer that has led to new ways of making products and services which can be widely benefited across the globe
- Reduction in inflation through a drastic fall in the manufacturing costs of production
- Potential increase in living standards of citizens of countries in favour of globalisation (although sadly not always the case, with exploitation occurring where regulation either fails or doesn't exist)
- Increase in immigration through rise in labour force movements across the globe

Negative consequences of globalisation:

- Lack of equal benefits to both developed and less economically developed countries, as global organisations tend to favour the developed economies more
- It widens the gap of inequality between the developing and developed world
- Failure of multi-national corporations to minimise risks to the environment and avoidance of any negative externalities and its consequent adverse effects on the nations from which they source for raw materials. These are mostly less developed economies
- Political antagonisms which have inclined to be against immigration and the loss of national identity

**Growing Economies**

Economic growth is achieved when the level of output of the country is increasing over a period of time. With such sustained rise in the output level, there are significant benefits which the citizens of the country will gain. There is a rise in the standard of living of the population. The real gross domestic product (GDP) is used to measure the growth in the economy of the country.

**Activity 58 – research the internet to see how the UK economy compares to emerging economies.**

www.economist.com/topics/emerging-markets

**Developments in emerging markets**

Emerging markets are markets which have characteristically low to middle income GDP per head. Countries that have been identified as emerging economies include the so called BRIC countries:

B - Brazil

R - Russia

I - India

C - China

Businesses need to develop the most effective strategies in order to enter emerging market. At the same time, due consideration must be given to the socio-political and economic climate of the country.

There are also MINT economies which are:

M – Mexico

I – Indonesia

N – Nigeria

T – Turkey

Economists are predicting that these will be the next high growth economies due to global location, increasing average incomes and an increase in western goods.

**Indicator of Growth – Human Development Index (HDI)**

The Human development index (HDI) is a statistical method used to rank countries by the level of human development. It is separated into:

- Very high human development
- High human development
- Medium human development
- Low human development

The human development index (HDI) is a measure of a number of factors:

- Life expectancy
- Literacy
- Education
- Standards of living

It is a standard means of measuring well-being, especially child welfare. It is used to distinguish if a given country is a developed, a developing or an under-developed nation. It is also used to measure the impact of economic policies on quality of life.

**Activity 59 –**

Log onto the United Nations and read about the HDI index.
http://hdr.undp.org/en/content/human-development-index-hdi

**International Trade and Business Growth**

Exports are where goods or services produced in one country are sent to another country for sale or trade. Imports are goods or service brought into a country from another.

Specialisation is where a country will concentrate on a product or service that they are best at or have plentiful as a natural resource. This gives the country or region a comparative advantage as they are able to produce the product or service at a lower cost than another country or region. An example of this is China, which has exported manufacturing goods where they have taken advantage of low labour costs.

**Activity 60 – research the internet and identify international and regional competitive advantages.**

Foreign Direct Investments (FDI) is a long-term investment in another country providing capital to help with economic development. This investment encourages the transfer of technology and skills between countries. It also enables the business making the FDI to promote its products more widely in the international markets.

For example, Dell computers are an US company that has factories in many other countries; these factories assemble personal customised computers for customers around the world.

Trade liberalisation is the removal or reduction in restrictions of the free trade of goods between countries. This includes tariff duties and surcharges and no tariff obstacles such as licensing rules and quotas. The benefits of trade liberalisation are that it encourages economic growth, increases efficiency and cost to the consumer (economies of scale). The drawback is that cheaper goods will enter the market that may not have the same quality and safety checks.

Globalisation has increased due to political changes in the collapse of communism and the opening of trade in the former communist countries. Developments in technology (ICT), communication and transport have increased the pace of globalisation. The internet has allowed 24 hour trade and e-commerce. Transport of containerised goods has meant vast amount of goods can be moved across the world at a low cost.

There has been a growth in multinational global brands for example Microsoft, Sony, Apple, McDonald's etc. Increased investment flows (FDI) has acted as a stimulus for globalisation, with organisations investing abroad. Migration, particularly in the European Union has increased where migrants have filled jobs and skill shortages in the UK. Another growth area for globalisation is structural change where there is a long-term shift in a country's economy. For example, a manufacturing economy may be transformed into a mixed economy.

## Protectionism

A country may want to restrict free trade (known as protectionism) to protect a new infant industry, protect employment, retain self-sufficiency, correct imbalances on the current account of the balance of payments or to protect strategic industries such as defence, essential foods, energy etc.

A country can do this by putting a tariff on imports, putting a limit on the quantity of imports, putting an embargo on goods, introducing a subsidy on domestic production to give a competitive advantage and putting administrative barriers to make it more difficult to trade.

The impact of protectionism is that there can be market distortion which may mean higher prices for the consumer as competition is distorted. Export subsidies can depress world prices which can damage outputs in developing countries. Production inefficiencies may occur as the lack of competition does not give an incentive to reduce costs.

**Activity 61 - Log onto the BBC web site and read the article on:**

'Protectionism is on its Way Back'
http://www.bbc.co.uk/news/business-18104024

**Trading Blocks**

There are several barriers to trade which restrict the free movement of goods and services across national boundaries. These barriers are enforced through the use of tariffs and quotas. Various measures to limit international trade include:

- Exchange controls
- Import Quotas
- Embargoes
- Export subsidies
- Tariffs
- Political reasons

Tariffs are the taxes which are imposed on the importation of goods into an economy. Import quotas are the restrictions which are physically used to limit the amount of importation of goods into an economy.

Trade barriers also exist in the form of pressures that are mounted to protect the developing nations which face large competition from large multinationals in the developed countries. Furthermore, infant industries which are young industries are protected through the use of tariffs because such industries are very small and unable to enjoy the benefits of economies of scale.

There are export subsidies that are offered by the developed countries in response to mounting pressure from developing economies from whom they largely depend upon for their exported produce. Such subsidies protect those in the farming and agricultural sectors.

There are conflicts of trade which arise due to the political, social and economic problems between countries. For instance, there are higher levels of free trade which exist between the USA and the European Union. However, this freedom of trade does not necessarily apply to other countries of the world.

Trading blocs have had a significant impact on the patterns of global trade. In the EU this has led to trade creation between the members who trade freely but to the adverse effect of countries outside of the EU. UK trade in manufactured goods has fallen as de-industrialisation takes place, but trade in commercial and financial services has increased. Trade in the former communist countries has increased their share in the world trade by taking advantage of low labour costs. China and India have increased their share of world trade by increasing manufacturing exports in clothing and technology goods.

**EU and the Single Market[2]**

The EU and the single market is the formation of a sole market by the members of the common market. It provides for free movement of labour, trade, capital and services. In addition to the benefits of the common market it also requires the following:

Common fiscal and monetary policies
Policy agreements on social, environmental, transport and regional issues

In February 1992, the move towards a single European market was strengthened by the Maastricht Treaty. This treaty served both economic and political objectives as it saw the member states unite in a move towards policies to strengthen their security and foreign policies.

---

[2] You should research the differences between the European Union and the Eurozone where the latter consists of countries from the EU which use the Euro as their currency, unlike the UK and others which are also within the EU but have retained their own currencies. http://europa.eu/about-eu/countries/member-countries/

**The European Central Bank**

This is the central bank of the European Union and is responsible for the setting of a common interest rate for the several countries which adopted the Euro as its currency. Furthermore, it manages the exchange rates of the Euro currency. This bank also has access to control part of the reserves of some of the member countries.

**The Euro**

There have been several merits and demerits of the Euro single currency. These have included:

- Enhancement of trade among member states
- The rise in more competitive markets and a greater level of price transparency
- Stability of the exchange rates
- Increase in foreign direct investment in member states

The demerits include:

- High interest rate levels by the European Central Bank
- Lack of corresponding economic growth of member states using the Euro in comparison to the growth of the United Kingdom which still has the pound sterling currency
- UK business could experience increase in transition costs by signing up to the Euro
- Virtually no control by member states of their domestic economic policy
- Loss of accountability to each member states electorate

These have been some of the arguments put forward for and against the adoption of the Euro single currency.

Over the years there has been a growth in the members of the European Union. Initially comprising six members, today the European Union has nearly thirty members; this has led to an increase in free trade, political stability and many more benefits.

The free trade agreement in South East Asian Nations is known as ASEAN which supports local manufacturing in all ASEAN countries. The aim of ASEAN is to have a competitive edge through the elimination of tariff and none tariff barriers also to attract foreign direct investment (FDI). NAFTA is a trade agreement between US, Canada and Mexico and aims to eliminate barriers to trade and investment with the removal of tariffs.

The advantages of trading blocs are:

- Free trade which encourages members to specialise and apply comparative advantage
- Access to markets meaning trade will increase
- Economies of scale
- Job creation
- Protection from cheaper imports
- The disadvantages of trading blocs are:
- Benefits of free trade are lost
- Distortion of trade
- Encourages inefficiency
- Trade disputes between trading agreements

**Activity 62 – Log onto the internet and read the article on the ASEAN free trade agreement.**

http://aseaninsight.economist.com/2015/04/06/trade-bloc-or-trade-block/

## Topic 4.2 - Global Markets and Business Expansion

### Learning Outcome

The aim of this section is for students to understand the following:

- Conditions That Prompt Trade
- Assessment of a Country as a Market
- Assessment of a Country as a Production Location
- Reasons for Global Mergers or Joint Ventures
- Global Competitiveness

**Conditions to Prompt Trade**

Organisations that have reached saturation point in the market they operate in or which face fierce competition, may wish to seek new opportunities internationally for their product. These are known as 'push factors' and can increase the product life cycle.

'Pull factors' are when an organisation is proactive to seek increased trade with the benefits of global economies of scale. The risk to the business is also spread across overseas markets in the event of business failure.

Outsourcing is when an organisation delegates the business function to a third party which may or may not be in another country. For example, the customer support of a large multinational organisation may be outsourced. The advantages of doing this are lower wages in an overseas country meaning a reduction in costs. The disadvantages are that standards are difficult to control and customer service can be affected as the delivery is not from the main organisation.

Off-shoring is the relocation of the business to another country such as manufacturing or customer services. The advantages are to reduce costs where wages may be lower in an overseas country. The disadvantages are control of quality, political and cultural barriers.

**Activity 63 - Research the following organisations:**

Outsourcing – Banks, Building Societies, Insurance companies
Off-shoring – Caterpillar, Ford Transit and Tata Steel
Log onto the internet and read the article about off-shoring and Birmingham County Council.
http://www.bbc.co.uk/news/business-13622189

**Assessment of a Country as a Market**

When an organisation is considering expanding overseas they need to assess the country and consider the following factors:

- Levels and growth of disposable income – is this sufficient to sell the product?
- Ease of doing business – what are the trade barriers?
- Infrastructure – are there any transport issues in the country?
- Political stability – is there any unrest or potential for this?
- Exchange rate – what is the rate against sterling?

**Assessment of a Country as a Production Location**

Another factor to consider is the change in location and the issues this can bring to the organisation:

- Cost of production – this is likely to be lower in China and India than in Europe.
- Skills and availability of the workforce – is there available labour and what is the skill level of this labour?
- Infrastructure – will there be any increased costs to move the products?
- Trading blocs – what are these in the Country?
- Government incentives – what are these in the Country?
- Ease of doing business – with a different country and culture?
- Political stability – will there be a change in government shortly?
- Natural resources – what are these in the Country?
- Return on Investment – what is this likely to be?
- Maintenance of quality – can this be assured?
- Shipping costs – will these bring the unit costs into line with UK manufacturing costs or will there still be an advantage financially
- Loss of UK goodwill – many consumers are reluctant to buy products manufactured in low cost countries despite their UK associations

Dependent on the industry this will bring different challenges and the levels of importance to the above.

**Reasons for Global Mergers or Joint Ventures**

A merger or a joint venture is where two organisations join together to form one. The advantages to this are:

- The risk is spread over different countries or regions, meaning that if there is business failure in an area, the organisation has other sections to the business.
- There are new markets, and there may be an advantage of a trading bloc.
- The organisation may be able to take advantage of an international brand or a patent to expand the business.
- Resources and supplies may be more readily available, taking advantage of economies of scale.
- The business will maintain and increase global competitiveness.

The disadvantages are:

- The organisation needs to be careful who they choose to merge with as this may not be a suitable match.
- Once the joint venture or merger has happened, it is difficult to back out.
- An example, of a joint venture is Sony-Ericsson which is a partnership between Japanese electronics and Swedish telecommunications.

**Activity 64 – Log onto the internet and read the BBC news article on this merger.**

http://news.bbc.co.uk/1/hi/business/1513112.stm

**Global Competitiveness**

The exchange rate will determine how competitive an organisation is. An increase in the exchange rate (appreciation) will mean foreign currency price is more expensive. A decrease in the exchange rate (depreciation) will mean that exports will be cheaper, and the organisation will be more competitive.

Competitive advantage can be achieved through cost leadership; this is a strategy to be the lowest-cost producer in the industry. Cost leadership is concerned with minimising costs by exploiting economies of scale. An organisation that has a large-scale business offering standard products, normally has this strategy.

Another way an organisation can have a competitive advantage is by differentiation of the product. The organisation strategy is to differentiate a small number of the target market segments; the product or service will be marketed as 'different' than any competitors' products and may be considered to be a niche product.

A threat to being competitive is the lack of skilled workers available for employment in an overseas organisation. If the organisation has a differentiation strategy with bespoke quality products, the workforce may not be available in all countries. This is where off-shoring or outsourcing may be a viable option.

**Activity 65 – Log onto the internet and read the article on global competitiveness in the US.**

http://www.economist.com/news/21566902-eight-point-plan-restore-american-competitiveness-what-washington-must-do-now

## Topic 4.3 - Global Marketing

### Learning Outcome

The aim of this section is for students to understand the following:

- Marketing
- Niche Markets
- Cultural and Social Factors

Global marketing is marketing on an international scale taking advantage of global opportunities to increase the profits of the business. This involves planning, producing, placing and promoting the organisations products worldwide. Global marketing is not just for the large multinational companies but can be relevant to small business through e-commerce. The phrase 'think global, act local' is often used to personalise marketing to the local market.

Organisations who market their products overseas often develop these to 'fit' into the local market; this is known as 'glocalisation' (a hideous combination of the words globalisation and localisation). Organisations use differentiation strategies to meet the requirements of the local market, but also need standardisation strategies to achieve economies of scale.

Marketing approaches that an organisation can adopt can be explored in the EPG model. This model looks at three elements: ethnocentrism, polycentrism and geocentrism. The purpose of the model is to create awareness and understanding of the marketing focus strategy for the business.

Ethnocentric focused organisations will have their headquarters in the home country where decisions are made from which concern the whole organisation. They will have high standards that control performance and quality of their products. An example of this is Wal-Mart who is an American organisation, although they own ASDA in the UK.

The advantages are that the organisation is simpler to operate and there is greater communication and control. The disadvantage is that there can be ineffective planning due to lack of consideration for local issues. There will be fewer innovations and there will be an inability to build a high quality local organisation.

Polycentrism-focused organisations have host country orientation and reflect the host countries local preferences. These organisations will vary their product to local market conditions. The advantages are exploitation of local markets, increased sales in the local market, host country government support and local managers with high morale. The disadvantages are that the cost of localised products will be high, there may be waste due to duplication of the product, and regard for local traditions can be at the expense of global growth.

A geocentric focused organisation has a worldwide marketing approach to management. This organisation has no preference for local or host country, and has the aim of best serving the organisation. The advantages are an integrated global outlook, better quality products, better utilisation of resources and improved local country management. The disadvantages are high communication and travel costs and slow decision making to take into account local issues.

Organisations such as Apple and Ferrari sell standardised products internationally, whereas Unilever adapt their products for the local markets. McDonald's fast food restaurant has an ethnocentric marketing strategy. For example, they now adapt their products to local markets appealing to local tastes such as the McSushi in China.

The 4Ps in marketing can be applied to global marketing as follows:

- PRICE – considerations for the exchange rate and global economy.
- PLACE – how good is the infrastructure of the Country?
- PRODUCT – does the product need adapting for the international market to consider cultural issues?
- PROMOTION – images and language may need to be adapted to prevent offence to a culture or religion.

Ansoff's Matrix can be applied for global marketing as follows:

- Market Penetration – market saturation in home country may mean further opportunities internationally.
- Market Development – focus on this as a growth strategy to enter the international market.
- Product Development – looking at different cultures in a country may mean developing a different product.
- Diversification – a new product may sell well in a new international market.
- Niche Markets

A niche market targets a small amount of sales where the product is significantly different to have a premium price. An organisation that produces a niche product should have high levels of customer service and customer loyalty.

An organisation that has niche products can better meet the needs of a range of different customer. A business that sells niche products can market themselves over several countries to generate sufficient sales to make a profit and be a viable business.

**Activity 66 - Research Dr Dre Headphones by Beats and design a global marketing campaign for this product. You should research YouTube and the target country for your marketing campaign.** http://uk.beatsbydre.com

**Cultural and Social Factors**

When a business markets their products internationally, the organisation needs to consider cultural differences and local customs that reflect the lifestyle and values of the people in the country. The products need to be adapted to market the product and not to cause offence.

Language translations can sometimes be misunderstood. For example, Coca-Cola product Diet Coke had negative connotations in Latin America and the brand was changed to 'Coke Lite'. The brown UPS delivery vans were the same as Spanish hearses and so the company changed the colour of the vans in this country. In an advertising campaign Pepsi used the slogan 'come alive with Pepsi'. In Taiwan this translated as 'bring your ancestors back from the dead'.

**Activity 67 - Research the internet for marketing blunders that have cultural and social factors.**

http://rudefoodnames.com

**Topic 4.4 - Global Industries and Companies (multinational corporations)**

**Learning Outcome**

The aim of this section is for students to understand the following:

- The Impact of MNCs
- Ethics
- Controlling MNCs

**Multinational Corporations**

Multinational Corporations (MNCs) are organisations that produce and sell goods in at least one country across the world. MNCs are likely to have offices and factories in different countries with a central head office to support the global management.

Examples of MNCs are JCB, GSK, Nike, Walmart, Coca-cola, Volkswagen, Toshiba, Apple, Tata etc.

The positives of a MNC are that they create jobs and wealth around the world; also they invest money in developing countries. The profits are used for research and development of the product, bring investment, improve technology and infrastructure in a country.

The negatives are that MNC often have a monopoly of power and make profits at the expense of the consumer. The market dominance often makes it difficult for smaller local business to survive. MNC have been criticised for using 'slave labour' by paying poor wage rates compared to Western standards. Considerations for the environment and pollution can also be secondary in the pursuit of profit.

**Activity 68 - Comment on the car manufacturer Ford motors that moved the production of cars and vans from the UK offshore to Turkey in 2013.**

http://www.dailyecho.co.uk/news/briefing/
http://www.dailyecho.co.uk/news/

**Ethics and Controlling MNC**

Ethics are the moral rights and wrongs of decisions that a business makes.

MNCs are coming under increased pressure to be ethical businesses, facing external pressure with increased scrutiny of business activities. External stakeholders such as pressure groups have used online media to highlight unethical practices of MNCs. In addition direct consumer action has been used to pressurise businesses to sell Fair Trade products.

A business cannot claim to be an ethical company if they ignore health, safety and environmental standards which may not be as stringent in developing countries. Also if they use child or forced labour in a sweatshop factory production, and violate basic worker rights.

The ethics of a business extend along the supply chain from suppliers, contractors, distributors and sales agents.

**Activity 69 - Log onto the internet and read the article on the Tata empire and ethics.**
http://www.independent.co.uk/news/business/analysis-and-features/what-makes-the-tata-empire-tick-10024897.html

Log onto the internet and read this article on the business ethics.
The dark underworld of Bangladesh's clothes industry
http://www.bbc.co.uk/news/world-asia-22306135